THE IRISH COAST TO COAST WALK

Knocknakilla Stone Circle above Millstreet Country Park

THE IRISH
COAST TO COAST WALK

by

PADDY DILLON

CICERONE PRESS
MILNTHORPE, CUMBRIA

© Paddy Dillon 1996
ISBN 1 85284 211 3
A catalogue record for this book is available from the British Library

Dedicated to the memory of
J.B. Malone

Advice to Readers

Readers are advised that whilst every effort is taken by the author to ensure the accuracy of this guidebook, changes can occur which may affect the contents. It is advisable to check locally on transport, accommodation, shops etc but even rights-of-way can be altered and, more especially overseas, paths can be eradicated by landslip, forest fires or changes of ownership.

The publisher would welcome notes of any such changes

Other Cicerone books by the same author:
    The Mountains of Ireland
    Walking the Galloway Hills
    Walking in the Northern Pennines
    Walking in County Durham

Front Cover: The Lack Road leads through a rugged valley
            near Glencar

CONTENTS

J.B.Malone's memorial stone at Luggala on the Wicklow Way

INTRODUCTION

Waymarked long distance walking routes are a relatively recent addition to the Irish countryside. The Wicklow Way was the first such trail to be fully marked and offered to walkers, and it can now be connected with other waymarked trails to offer an almost complete Coast to Coast Walk across Ireland from Dublin to the Atlantic coastline of Co Kerry.

Much of the credit for initiating the development of the waymarked trail network must go to the late J.B. Malone - often referred to as the "Walking Encyclopaedia". JB took to the hills in 1931 and contributed walking articles to the *Evening Herald* from 1938 to 1975. The Wicklow Mountains were the hills he knew and loved the best, and in 1966 he prepared a plan for a route which was to become the Wicklow Way. The original plan actually envisaged a circular walk, but Cospoir (the National Sports Council) became involved in the development of walking routes and the Wicklow Way became linear so that it could link with a proposed South

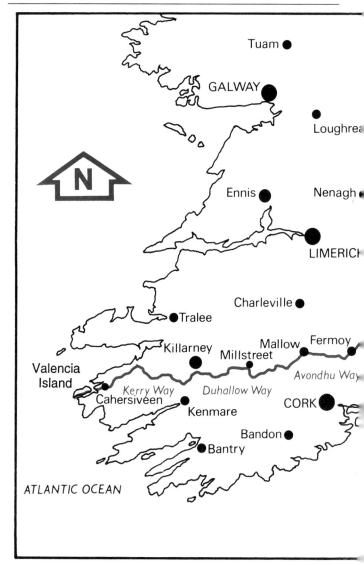

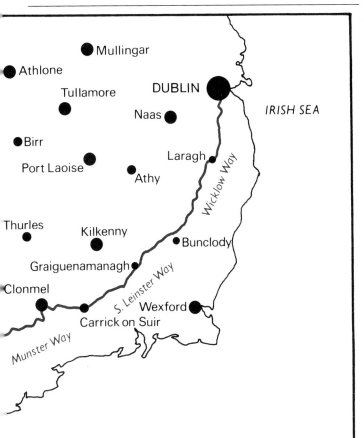

Mullingar

Athlone

Tullamore

DUBLIN

IRISH SEA

Naas

Birr

Laragh

Wicklow Way

Port Laoise

Athy

Thurles

Kilkenny

Bunclody

Graiguenamanagh

S. Leinster Way

Clonmel

Wexford

Carrick on Suir

Munster Way

A COAST TO COAST
OF IRELAND

Leinster Way. The South Leinster Way was in turn planned to join a route called the Munster Way, which was planned to stretch across country to link with the Kerry Way. In 1982 the Wicklow Way was declared open and the other routes began to open in turn. JB was appointed as Field Officer by Cospoir and he was closely involved in the development of all the early waymarked trails. His memorial stone has been planted above Luggala in the Wicklow Mountains and he is recorded as the "Pioneer of the Wicklow Way".

Problems with the waymarked trails began to arise almost immediately. Following extensive media coverage, large numbers of walkers took to the Wicklow Way, so that some of the boggier parts became badly overtrodden. Strategically important bridges in Glencree and at the Watergates were swept away in floods, while loose waymark posts were either uprooted by vandals or accidentally run over by heavy forestry vehicles. The committees which helped to establish routes such as the South Leinster Way and Muster Way fell apart soon after blazing those trails, so that no-one was available to address maintenance issues. More seriously, problems concerning Occupier's Liability arose. Put simply, walkers injuring themselves on a waymarked trail could, in theory, sue the landowner for damages. Disputes arose about who would cover the insurance costs for each of the trails, and indemnify the landowners against any potential claims for injuries. Given the complicated nature of these problems, the development of the trail network ground to a halt for a couple of years.

Insurance, liability and maintenance issues have all been addressed in recent years and new trails have been blazed across country to bring the Irish Coast to Coast Walk close to completion. Extensions to the Munster Way were titled the Avondhu Way and Duhallow Way. There are unmarked gaps to either side of the Duhallow Way, but it is likely that further links will be forged in the future. The Duhallow Way is fairly close to the Kerry Way, which visits a number of points on the Atlantic coast. In effect, therefore, there is almost a completely waymarked Coast to Coast Walk across Ireland from Dublin to the Kerry coast. If Valencia Island is taken as a terminus, then the total distance across country is 370 miles (594km). Given that most of the trails have been routed across fairly gentle countryside, often using firm surfaces, walkers can adopt a

Standard waymarked trail logo - sometimes only showing the arrow

spanking pace and should be able to cover the distance over three weeks if they are used to walking long distances. This guide offers walkers basic information about the course of the Coast to Coast Walk, and the facilities available along the way. It needs to be used in conjunction with the recommended Ordnance Survey maps which are now being updated in a detailed 1:50,000 format.

GETTING TO AND FROM IRELAND

Rail/Sail: There is no point bringing a vehicle with you on the Coast to Coast Walk, except if you require some form of back-up for a group walk or record-breaking attempts. There are rail services to Holyhead in North Wales, from where ferries will transport you to either Dublin or Dun Laoghaire. A handy tip - Youth Hostel Association membership cards from around the world will qualify their holders for a 25% discount on the foot passenger fare when produced at the ferryports. Once in Dublin or Dun Laoghaire, all you need to do is to sort out your accommodation for the night, or if you have arrived on a night sailing, immediately embark upon the walk first thing in the morning. Travellers from Scotland may use rail services to Stranraer, then take a ferry to either Larne or Belfast, before another train ride continues southwards to Dublin. Anyone arriving from the South of England or South Wales can catch a train to either Pembroke or Fishguard, then use ferries to reach Rosslare, and travel northwards by train to Dublin. Continental visitors can use ferry services from Cherbourg or Le Havre to Rosslare before taking a train to Dublin, though visitors from Northern Europe could use Britain as an enormous "stepping stone" on the way to Ireland.

Flights: There are numerous flights into Dublin from the London airports, provincial airports around Britain, and from many European capitals also. A frequent bus links Dublin Airport with the city centre. At the end of the Coast to Coast Walk, it is possible to fly out from Kerry County Airport at Farranfore, either stopping at Dublin for further connections, or occasionally flying direct to airports in Britain. Your travel agent will be able to advise on specific flight schedules.

Package Deals: One of the few tour operators capable of handling all the necessary transport, accommodation, maps and insurance cover for a route such as the Coast to Coast Walk is Enjoy Ireland, Ainsworth Street, Blackburn, Lancashire BB1 6AZ, England (tel. 01254 692889). All they would need to know from prospective walkers are the intended dates of travel and a list of places where accommodation is required.

GETTING AROUND IRELAND

Dublin Bus operates frequent services to all parts of the capital, while DART trains run frequently around Dublin Bay and offer a speedy link between Dun Laoghaire and the city centre. Moving beyond Dublin, most bus services are operated by Bus Eireann, who produce an annually revised paperback book of timetables. On many parts of the Coast to Coast Walk, bus services are sparse, so it is important to check the *table numbers* in the Bus Eireann guide to be sure of the exact days and times of services. In some areas there may be seasonal variations, or no Sunday services. On a walk such as the Coast to Coast Walk, you may not even need to use a bus, but if you intend splitting the walk over two or three separate holidays, then you may need to know how to get to and from particular places along the way. Buses may also prove useful for short journeys off-route in search of lodgings. There are only a handful of towns with railway stations along the Coast to Coast Walk, and timetables can be checked with Iarnrod Eireann.

It may interest walkers to know that the town of Clonmel is roughly situated at the halfway point of the Coast to Coast Walk, and it boasts both a railway station and a comprehensive range of bus services. Portmagee, on the other hand, at the end of the Coast to Coast Walk, has no scheduled public transport and you may have to make private taxi arrangements before leaving Cahersiveen on the last day's walk. Bus services from Cahersiveen can be tied in with further services from Killarney, or link with a train from Killarney or a flight from Kerry County Airport at Farranfore. As you will appreciate, if time is running out towards the end of the Coast to Coast Walk, a missed connection as you are trying to get home could prove disastrous.

TOURIST INFORMATION

Bord Failte is the national tourism organisation and there are also closely allied regional tourism organisations. Each organisation operates Tourist Information Offices and you will also find small, locally supported Tourist Information Points. Generally, these places should be able to help you with any accommodation bookings or public transport queries. They may even have maps and guidebooks on sale, but don't expect them to be able to offer specific route directions to passing walkers. Towns which have Tourist Information Offices are noted in the text, though there are only a handful of them along the Coast to Coast Walk.

MONEY MATTERS

The official currency of the Republic of Ireland is the Irish pound, or *punt*. Cash, cheques and major credit cards are widely accepted in Ireland, though as you will be travelling largely through quiet and unsophisticated rural areas where your spending is likely to be small-scale, you should give some thought to your monetary needs. Usually, it is possible for overseas visitors to pass off their own currency on their first bus-ride into Dublin from the airport or ferryport, but this relies on the goodwill of the driver or conductor. Once in Dublin, you really should obtain some hard cash before setting off walking. A bank or bureau de change can be visited at the outset, though foreign currency cheques may need to be backed by a Eurocheque card or other guarantee. Travellers' cheques are easily changed. In some remote places, where you may be far from a bank, some pubs or hotels may change money for you, but the rate of exchange is likely to be unfavourable for you. Notes in common usage include £20, £10 and £5. Coins include £1, 50p, 20p, 10p, 5p, 2p and 1p. Most coins, but not the £1 or 20p, will look familiar in size, shape and colour to those used by British visitors. With the banknotes, be aware that there are forged notes in circulation, so make yourself familiar with each note in turn and take care over any transactions you may make in dimly lit shops and pubs.

PASSPORTS

With the lifting of all sorts of economic and political barriers, there is virtually free movement for EU citizens through all EU member states. Travel between Britain and Ireland has long been a casual and passport-free affair - but only for Irish and British citizens. If travelling from the Continent, or further afield, you should check requirements with the Irish embassy in your home country, as you may require both a passport and visa, and you would need to make allowance for this when making your travel plans. In any case, everyone should carry some ready form of identification for spot security checks at points of entry and departure. International terrorism and drug smuggling remain worldwide problems.

ACCOMMODATION

You should always be aware of what accommodation options you can expect for at least a couple of days in advance. While it is indeed possible to book all your overnights before setting out, it does mean that you are tied to a rather rigid schedule. You can try turning up on the doorsteps of B&Bs unannounced, but you run the risk of finding all the beds occupied at popular times of the year, or all the accommodation closed during the off-peak season. An accommodation list is provided at the end of the guide which gives the names and addresses of various hotels, guesthouses, B&Bs and hostels which are handy for walkers on the Coast to Coast Walk. These are nearly all approved by Bord Failte, or are listed as "specialist accommodation" which may be rather more basic, but is nevertheless close to the route. Bord Failte publish an annual listing of addresses and give the appropriate prices and facilities.

Most of the places listed in this guide are homely B&Bs, with a few hotels and a scattering of hostels. You should note that a couple of stops on the Wicklow Way offer *only* hostel accommodation, and in a couple of other places, notably along the Duhallow Way, lodgings are particularly limited. If you do your reading and phoning a couple of days in advance, then you will have the necessary flexibility to enjoy the walk at your own pace, while still having the security of your accommodation waiting for you. If a particular address is a little way off-route, you could try asking for a lift from an appropriate point at a convenient time, as some people will be quite happy to help you out if they are able. Similarly, people can be surprisingly helpful even when all their beds are occupied, and will sometimes go to some length to make sure that you do in fact find a place for the night.

COAST TO COAST GEOLOGY

Coast to Coast walkers travel rapidly from the urban lowlands to the Wicklow wilderness and cover some of the toughest terrain in the first few days of the journey. The Wicklow Mountains and neighbouring Blackstairs Mountains are part of a vast intrusion of granite which takes a week to walk across! The course of the Wicklow Way meanders between the granite massif and the shiny schistose rock which surrounds it. The shist was formed when the molten mass of granite was intruded into the existing ancient Ordovician bedrock, altering the bedrock by a process of tremendous heat and pressure known as metamorphism. Kippure, Mullaghcleevaun and Tonelagee are granite, while Djouce Mountain and Croaghanmoira are schist. Lugnaquillia is unusual, because it is mostly granite, but it has retained its original "roof" of schist. On the whole, the granite uplands form vast, rounded, whaleback hills, while the schist tends to weather into more shapely peaks and has been excavated into deep glens between the mountains.

After passing Graiguenamanagh, the landscape of the South Leinster Way is dominated by the "Three Sisters" - the rivers Barrow, Nore and Suir. All three rivers appear to chart curious courses and have apparently carved their ways through whole ranges of hills and mountains. Opinions are divided as to whether these rivers have been "superimposed" on the landscape after wearing down through long-vanished upper layers of rock; or whether they display "antecedent drainage" and have simply kept to their original courses despite any uplifting of the strata through geological time.

The Comeragh Mountains and Knockmealdown Mountains are formed of Old Red Sandstone - vast thicknesses of Devonian sands and grits which have been crumpled and contorted by immense pressures through the ages. In fact, this sort of strata is crossed by the Munster Way, Avondhu Way, Duhallow Way and Kerry Way. Of particular interest is a feature known as the Armorican Front, which is the line dividing the predominantly Old Red Sandstone massif from the predominantly Carboniferous Limestone of the lowlands. You can look along this line and see the division clearly between the Knockmealdown Mountains and the River Suir, between the Nagles Mountains and the River Blackwater, and between the Derrynasaggart Mountains and the lowlands around Millstreet, Rathmore and Barraduff. You would hardly be aware of the Carboniferous Limestone, which dominates so much of central Ireland, and the route steers clear of classic features such as Mitchelstown Cave and Crag Cave. However, an exploration of the shore of Muckross Lake in the Killarney National Park reveals this limestone at its water-worn best.

All the mountain groups crossed on the Coast to Coast Walk feature typical corrie lakes and "U" shaped glacial valleys, but in the mountains of Kerry these are particularly well developed. The Kerry Way proceeds through the glacial Black Valley and ice-scoured corries can be seen along the flanks of the MacGillycuddy's Reeks and other mountain ranges. Only rarely do current winter conditions remind walkers of the last Ice Age, as snow and ice seldom lie long on the Kerry mountains and are quickly removed by warm, damp Atlantic airflows.

WEATHER

Ireland's proximity to the Atlantic Ocean guarantees that an almost constant westerly airflow will bring warm, damp air over the country. Between 150 and 200 depressions track generally north of Ireland each year, so that frontal systems sweep regularly across the countryside. Each system is likely to bring rain, but there will generally be clear spells in between, when the countryside shows off vibrant colours. As a general rule of thumb you can assume that March, April and May will be fairly dry and clear, though you may catch the tail-end of winter on the hills. In June, July and August you could expect showers, or even thunderstorms with the increasing heat and humidity. Flies can become a nuisance in these conditions and some insect repellent should be carried and used. There is sometimes a possibility of good walking weather around September and October, though the clear, cool and dry spells may be quite short-lived. The winter months are characterised by a drop in temperature, with more rain and a possibility of some snow or sharp frosts. However, because of the oceanic influences, summers and winters are not so markedly different as they are in Britain or on the Continent, where extremes are more likely. In Ireland, a week of sunny weather might be classed as a heatwave, but it also gives rise to a thick heat-haze which dulls the surrounding colours of the countryside. Snow can sometimes fall to some depth, particularly on the Wicklow Mountains, but it seldom lasts long, except for small pockets in hollows on the hills.

Overall, you should expect all sorts of weather conditions to arrive in an apparently haphazard manner. Even on a simple day-walk you could experience striking variations. You need to pack your waterproofs and you will certainly need to wear them at some point on the journey from Coast to Coast. You should also take care when the sun shines as the air can be crystal clear and cool breezes may give you little indication that you are becoming sunburnt. Pack some suncream and be ready to use it. As rain is often accompanied by low cloud and mist on the hills, you should be prepared to navigate using a map and compass if necessary. Although there are no accurately predictable long-range weather forecasts for Ireland, the day-to-day forecasts are often quite reliable. Try and tune into a radio, or catch a forecast on the television each evening, so that you can prepare yourself mentally and physically for conditions likely to be experienced on the following day.

FLORA AND FAUNA

Given the tremendous range of landscapes and habitats along the Coast to Coast Walk, any attempt to catalogue the species which might be noted along the way would degenerate into a mere list in the space available. However, you could pack a copy of the *Wicklow Way Natural History Field Guide*, by Ken Boyle and Orla Bourke, published by Cospoir. This indicates the range of flora and fauna which was noted over twelve months on the northern stretch of the Wicklow Way. As the terrain, and hence the range of wildlife habitats, varies from forest to upland morlands and lowland glens, you would find that similar conditions would be repeated across Ireland.

In general terms, the uplands display open heathery slopes and blanket bogs, which often support patches of bilberry or wiry moor grass where the ground is dry. Sodden ground conditions allow bright patches of sphagnum moss to form. Hares and foxes will run even to these heights, while grouse find cover in the heather. Ravens and other birds of prey may be seen wheeling overhead in search of smaller mammals. Lonely pools of water serve to attract migrating wildfowl. As the uplands give way to the glens, heather may give way to invasive bracken and clumps of yellow-flowered, coconut-scented gorse. The more cultivated lowland glens and riversides may support a range of crops, but more likely it will be given over to grass to pasture sheep and cattle. Rabbits sometimes occur in great number, and the bird-life will be profuse. Although occasional stands of oak, ash, beech and alder may be passed, most trees outside of small woods and hedgerows will be commercial plantings and include fast-growing spruces, pines and firs. When these are closely planted, little light reaches the forest floor, which may simply be a sterile mat of dead needles. However, such plantations do offer good cover to red deer and sika deer throughout the Wicklow Mountains, and both species are spreading further afield. You may spot them at dawn and dusk grazing along the forest margins. Migrant birds such as crossbills have specially adapted beaks for teasing nuts from pine cones, and seskins also prefer coniferous cover.

Early summer is the best time to enjoy the bulk of the wild flowers, which bring a riot of colour to the hedgerows, riverbanks and roadside verges. Later in the summer, the heather takes on a purple flush in the hills, while autumn tints change practically from day to day in deciduous woods and on bracken covered slopes. This can be a good time for spotting migrant birds. Fungi may also be producing their strangely shaped fruiting bodies around the same time. While the *Wicklow Way Natural History Field Guide* will actually serve you well for most of the Coast to Coast Walk, the Kerry countryside in particular is populated by species deserving a special mention. Pure Irish red deer inhabit the "Wilderness" on the slopes of Mangerton Mountain, while the Kerry Spotted Slug is a curious creature you may observe grazing after heavy rain. Floral tributes include species with a peculiar worldwide distribution, in that they occur naturally only in south-west Ireland and the Pyrenees, or around the Mediterranean. These include the saxifrage known as St Patrick's Cabbage (or London Pride), the Arbutus (or Strawberry Tree), and the blue-flowered insectivorous Greater Butterwort.

In the winter months, by the Upper Lake in the Killarney National Park, a flock of White Fronted Geese from Greenland may be grazing, and this may result in a diversion of the course of the

Kerry Way. Only towards the very end of the Coast to Coast Walk do seabirds really make an impression, but time spent on Valencia Island's Bray Head will reveal a host of species. In fact, a cruise to the Skellig Islands will reveal gannets, and in season, puffins too.

ACCESS TO THE COUNTRYSIDE

The waymarked trails which make up the Coast to Coast Walk have been pieced together from various paths, tracks and roads. Whenever possible, the roads which are used are fairly quiet, narrow minor roads. Generally, all types of traffic are permitted along such roads, unless they are simply too narrow or have a bridge with a specific weight limit. Paths and tracks through the countryside may be rights of way - over which foot travellers may freely pass - but in many instances access has been negotiated for walkers. Generally, the routes which have been negotiated do not become rights of way, but the landowner grants a "wayleave". This can be withdrawn by the landowner at any time, and it may need to be renewed after a period of years.

The granting of a wayleave can involve certain conditions having to be fulfilled, such as a ban on camping or dogs. It is therefore important that walkers following the waymarked trails behave considerately at all times and remember that the land they are crossing is someone's livelihood. Don't take dogs on the trails, and avoid disturbing livestock. Be sure to close gates and cross stiles carefully to avoid damage to fences. Don't pollute watercourses, light fires or leave litter. Camping is expressly forbidden in state forests and National Parks, but many landowners would gladly allow the use of a field corner if they were approached with a polite request. The trails are generally not supposed to be used by cycle-riders or horse riders, except where such use is already established. Nor are mass sponsored walks encouraged as heavy use in a short period can lead to considerable damage in places.

Insurance cover has been provided for the waymarked trails - mainly to indemnify landowners from potential claims made against them by walkers injuring themselves. To be fair, your personal safety is really your own responsibility while you are walking through the countryside, and this forms the core of the Occupier's Liability Act of 1995.

ROUTE FINDING

Waymarks almost universally bear a "walking man" logo and this may appear on both waymark posts and roadside signposts. Generally, an arrow will show the direction you are supposed to take as either left, right, or straight on (pointing upwards for the latter). Some waymark posts may simply bear an arrow, and not use the "walking man" logo. However, there is more to route finding along the Coast to Coast Walk than simply following arrows. In some areas the waymarking is particularly sparse. Waymark posts can also be knocked over, either accidentally or on purpose, and they may be replaced the wrong way round. Signposts are also prey to being spun around the wrong way - often by mischievous children! There are also gaps between some of the trails, where a suggested stretch of road-walking will not be waymarked. To be sure of staying on course, you should look on the waymarks as simply confirming that you are still on course. Be a bit suspicious if you haven't seen a marker for some time, and check your map against the guidebook to see if you are still on course. The notes in this guidebook need to be used in conjunction with the appropriate maps, and the sketch maps really only show the general direction of the route.

MAP COVERAGE

The entire course of the Coast to Coast Walk is covered by Half Inch to One Mile maps (1:126,720 scale). These have several drawbacks - their small scale, cluttered appearance, insufficient detail and dated information being among them. Unfortunately, you may be forced to use them in some places as there aren't any real alternatives. None of the Half Inch maps shows the waymarked trails, so you will need to study them carefully alongside the guidebook before each

Signposts often indicate placenames in both Irish and English

day's walk, as well as referring to them during the day. The good news is that the Half Inch maps are gradually being replaced by excellent 1:50,000 scale maps. Although these don't quite yet offer a complete Coast to Coast coverage, they certainly offer splendid detail in some areas. Established routes such as the Wicklow Way and Kerry Way are clearly marked on the new maps, and new trails are being added as new maps are published.

Although not all the 1:50,000 maps have been published, the relevant sheet numbers are given at the start of every day's walk, so that if they become available you can simply buy the appropriate sheet number. Only a few areas are covered at a scale of 1:25,000 - the Ordnance Survey have published maps of Killarney National Park and MacGillycuddy's Reeks on the Kerry Way. A map/guide at the same scale is available covering part of the Wicklow Way around Glendalough, and this is on offer from the Glendalough Visitor Centre. The 1:25,000 Comeragh Mountains map/guide covers a good stretch of the Munster Way and is published privately. Each of the daily stretches in this guide begins with a list of appropriate maps, which you can either obtain from larger bookshops or some Tourist Information Offices. They can be obtained direct from the Ordnance Survey of Ireland, Phoenix Park, Dublin 8, Ireland.

SAFETY

Most of the Coast to Coast Walk runs across Ireland at a low level. When following minor roads, be sure to walk on the right-hand side of the road and face oncoming traffic. Motorists tend to be most considerate of pedestrians, slowing down noticeably and giving them wide berth in passing. Any problems on stretches of road-walking can be sorted out simply by flagging down a car, or asking for help at the nearest house or farm. In state forests, the biggest problem is that of becoming completely disorientated and losing your way. If this happens, you should try and retrace your steps to a point where you were quite sure of your position, then try again. Never make the mistake of trying to short-cut between the densely-packed trees, or cutting across clear-felled slopes, as these moves can prove most exhausting and debilitating.

In upland country, take great care over navigation - especially in mist. Use your map and compass carefully and be prepared for cold, wet weather. You should also take precautions against summer heat in open country, packing sufficient fluid and suncream for protection against dehydration and sunburn. You should always carry protective clothing, and a complete change of clothes, as well as enough food and drink to see you through each day's walk. Extra supplies are necessary in case you have to spend a night out in the open. In remote places, a first aid kit, and first aid knowledge, is essential to deal with any cuts, sprains or broken bones which might occur by accident. If help is needed to evacuate a casualty from the hills, then someone has to get to a telephone and alert the Gardai (Police) by dialling 999. They will then call out the Mountain Rescue, or arrange a helicopter airlift as appropriate. With care, however, there is no reason why such a situation should arise in the first place. A bit of common sense goes a long way towards heading off accidents and injuries.

THE SCHEDULE

The Coast to Coast Walk is broken down into manageable lengths based on the availability of accommodation. The route is presented as a 21 day walk covering 370 miles (594km). This gives a daily average of about $17^1/_2$ miles ($28^1/_4$km). There is an awkward day measuring 25 miles (40km), but it is possible to break this into two halves at a farmhouse B&B. The individual trails are presented each in their turn - the Wicklow Way, South Leinster Way, Munster Way, Avondhu Way, Duhallow Way and Kerry Way. With unmarked road-links, the Coast to Coast Walk stretches from the tidal River Liffey in the centre of Dublin to Valencia Island on the Atlantic coast of Kerry. Walkers who cannot spare three weeks for the walk can conveniently split the distance into two roughly equal halves by breaking off at Clonmel and resuming the walk at a later date. There is an excellent choice of bus and train services to and from Clonmel, which proves quite useful.

THE WICKLOW WAY

> ## DAY 1:
> ## *Dublin to Marlay Park*
> ### *(Sketch map 1)*

Distance:	7 miles (11km).
Maps:	OS 1:50,000 Sheet 50
	OS 1:63,360 Map of Dublin District.
	OS 1:126,720 Sheet 16.
	OS 1:20,000 Map of Greater Dublin.

The River Liffey is tidal all the way through the centre of Dublin, so the Coast to Coast Walk can start on O'Connell Bridge, which is one of the main thoroughfares of the capital. The waymarked Wicklow Way starts on the outskirts of Dublin, at Marley Park, so the first day's walk is a suggested way from O'Connell Bridge to the park. Purists might like to start by dipping their feet in the waters of the Liffey. They may, with care, descend slippery steps at the side of O'Connell Bridge on Aston Quay and perform this ritual, then the walk can commence towards the distant Kerry coast!

Walk southwards from O'Connell Bridge along Westmorland Street, passing between the Bank of Ireland's columns and the railings of Trinity College to reach Grafton Street. The latter part of Grafton Street is pedestrianised and is lined with a full range of shops. Entertainment is provided by street artists and buskers before you reach the corner of St Stephen's Green. You can enter the park by passing through an impressive gateway, but keep close to the western side to emerge at another corner gateway and continue along Harcourt Street. Turn right around the Wang offices, then turn left along Richmond Street South. This will bring you to the Grand Canal at Portobello, where there is a bridge and a lock.

Don't cross the canal, but turn right and follow a path alongside it to the next bridge westwards. Cross over this bridge and continue along Harold's Cross Road. There is a small park you could walk through - a triangle of trees and flower beds between two busy roads - but be sure to continue along Harold's Cross Road and on into Terenure Road North. When you reach the main crossroads at Terenure, go along Rathfarnham Road, which crosses the River Dodder before reaching Rathfarnham Castle. Keep left into Grange Road, which itself suddenly turns right and passes the impressive gateway of the Loreto Abbey.

Follow Grange Road until you can turn right onto Sarah Curran Avenue and enter St Enda's Park at a gateway. Keep to the right inside the park until you reach a small stream, then turn left and follow any paths which trace this waterway upstream. Later, another left turn leads alongside the park wall, then you go through a narrow gateway to emerge back on Grange Road again. Continue along Grange Road, which immediately bears left, to reach the gates of Marlay Park and the beginning of the Wicklow Way. You could launch straight into this waymarked trail, but you should realise that there is no accommodation until distant Knockree Youth Hostel. There is no accommodation close to Marlay Park either, but Dublin Bus 47B will take you back into the centre of Dublin if required, where you can avail of everything from hostel to hotel accommodation. In the morning, you need to catch the same bus from Hawkins Street to return to Marlay Park.

Dublin's Fair City
If you want to make a thorough exploration of Dublin, then you will need a week to spare before you even think about the Coast to Coast Walk! It was sited on the River Liffey over a thousand years ago by the Vikings, so there is plenty of accumulated history. If you are only interested in brief details of things which are immediately apparent from the walk, then a few minutes at each of the following points shouldn't cause any unnecessary delay.

O'Connell Bridge
Named after Daniel O'Connell, whose monument can be seen just across on the north side of the bridge. He was born in 1775 and became a distinguished and active barrister and politician. He formed the Catholic Association in 1823, which became a popular

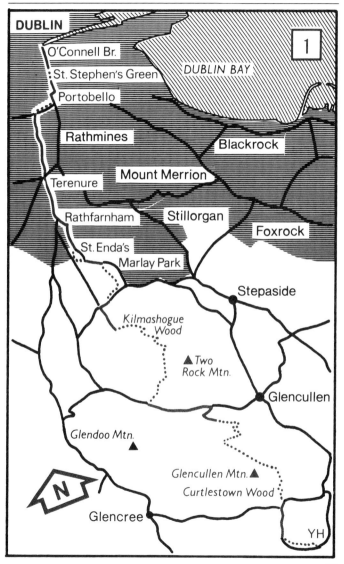

O'Connell Bridge in Dublin spans the tidal River Liffey at the start

and influential movement which, guided by O'Connell, was a force which led to the Catholic Emancipation of 1829. He was also instrumental in moves towards the repeal of the Act of Union of 1800. He earned the title of "The Liberator" and is currently featured on the £20 note. The four angelic figures surrounding his pedestal symbolise Eloquence, Courage, Fidelity and Patriotism. Holes in their wings were caused by flying bullets during the Easter Rising of 1916, which was centred on the nearby General Post Office. The Coast to Coast Walk later passes the birthplace of O'Connell, on the Kerry coast at Cahersiveen, some 355 miles (570km) distant as the waymarked trails run!

Westmoreland Street
If you can stop for a moment without obstructing the crowds, then look up from shop level and marvel at the varied architecture of the upper stories of the buildings. Styles include Italian, Dutch and French all side-by-side. Note also the old facade which has been incorporated into the reflective glass frontage of the Educational Building Society. Across the road is Bewley's, where you should

consider a break for tea or coffee. Apparently, you haven't *been* to Dublin if you haven't been to Bewley's!

The Bank of Ireland

Originally built as the House of Parliament, but used by the Bank of Ireland since the Act of Union of 1800. It has a striking, circular form supported on all sides by columns. It can be entered via impressive porticos and there can be no finer place to conduct a financial transaction - under a chandelier near a blazing fire! Bureau de change facilities are available for visiting walkers. The former House of Lords retains much of its original form and this part of the building can be inspected at certain times.

Trinity College

Founded by Queen Elizabeth I in 1592 and passed in only a few seconds. It takes all day to explore properly, but you could at least walk in through the gateway and tread the "hallowed cobbles" - passing from the busy city streets into an oasis of industrious calm. The Book of Kells is housed in the Old Library and one of its lavishly illuminated pages is turned every day to be viewed by a long queue of visitors. The college is also entitled, under the Copyright Act, to one copy of every book published in the British Isles - including this one! There is an audio-visual exhibition if you have the time to spare, as well as art exhibitions and the annual Trinity Ball.

Molly Malone

A sculpture of Molly Malone, complete with wheelbarrow, cockles, mussels, etc. She stands halfway along Grafton Street between the crawling traffic and the pedestrianised section. Often surrounded by street artists, who give way to buskers and even classy string quartets as you pass along the street. Jugglers and magicians may also be performing and you may even catch a few verses of street poetry before reaching St Stephen's Green.

St Stephen's Green

A large, rectangular park in the care of the Office of Public Works. In fact, their office actually overlooks the green. It was enclosed in the late 17th century, but it wasn't finally landscaped until 1877, by

Arthur Guinness - the brewer of the "black stuff" closer to Phoenix Park. St Stephen's Green is richly ornamental and well used by the citizens of Dublin for rest and enjoyment. Arrive too early in the day, however, and the gates will be closed, but you can walk alongside the railings in that case.

The Grand Canal
The Grand Canal runs from Dublin's Ringsend Basin to the mighty River Shannon at Shannon Harbour in Co Offaly. There is a continuous towpath, which is fully waymarked for walkers beyond the city and allows a splendid, easy, low-level, cross-country walk of some 80 miles (130km). This particular stretch at Portobello was constructed in 1790. The Grand Canal can offer an alternative start to the Coast to Cast Walk, as the waymarked towpath of both the Grand Canal Way and the Barrow Way can be combined to offer a low-level route from Dublin to Graiguenamanagh in Co Kilkenny. The Wicklow Way and the South Leinster Way are linked in this guide to provide a walk mainly through hill country to reach Graiguenamanagh.

Rathfarnham Castle
This castle has a fairly nondescript exterior, but had been in continuous occupation from 1585 until 1985. It was finally purchased by the state in 1987 after being vacated by the Jesuits. It is currently undergoing restoration and should eventually become a fine attraction in the neighbourhood.

St Enda's Park
The centre-piece of St Enda's Park is the former St Enda's School founded by Patrick Pearse. The school, which had its lessons taught through the medium of Irish, opened in 1908 but suffered financial problems. Pearse was involved in the nationalist struggle and allowed the house and grounds to be used for covert military activities. It was Pearse who read out the Declaration of the Republic from the steps of the General Post Office on O'Connell Street - an act which was to lead to his execution shortly afterwards at Kilmainham Jail. St Enda's now houses some of Pearse's effects and the whole park is managed by the Office of Public Works. Make sure you

arrive well before dusk to be able to walk through the park grounds, and check specific opening times for the house.

DAY 2:
Marlay Park to Knockree
(Sketch map 1)

Distance: 14 miles (22km).

Maps: OS 1:50,000 Sheets 50 and 56.
OS 1:63,360 Map of Dublin District and Map of Wicklow District.
OS 1:126,720 Sheet 16.

The gates of Marlay Park on Grange Road are opened at 10am every morning. Arrive any earlier than this and you'll either have to wait for them to open, or walk around the boundary wall instead. A Wicklow Way mapboard stands inside the grounds by a car park close to Marlay House. Another very detailed map shows the layout of the park grounds. Follow a tarmac path away from the car park, across close-cropped lawns, then branch off to the right to follow a path through a narrow strip of woodland alongside a small stream. There are ornamental ponds to pass, a variety of trees and occasional sculptures such as the "Four Seasons" along the way. There is a right turn along a broader path which runs roughly parallel to the park boundary wall. The path passes alongside sports fields before reaching another mapboard by a small car park. Exit from the park at this point to reach a minor road outside.

Turn right to follow the road downhill, then turn left just before reaching a bridge at the bottom. Another left turn leads up Kilmashogue Lane, passing the ruins of an old mill and later climbing past a modern thatched house. Keep going uphill until there is a left turn into Kilmashogue Wood, where there is a small car park. Take the middle one of three possible tracks leaving the car park. The forest track runs gradually uphill, with occasional views out of the trees across the Garda Siochana Golf Course. Gaps in the trees frame various urban or coastal features. The track zig-zags uphill and you should later watch out for a turning on the right, where a steep and stony path climbs uphill. Walkers missing this turning will find themselves heading towards a series of masts on the slopes of Three Rock Mountain.

The steep and stony path climbs high into the forest and offers a much wider view across the urban sprawl of Dublin, as well as around Howth and further along the coast. The distant Mountains of Mourne may feature far to the north. Towards the top of the path there is a curious right and left turn, where in retrospect you'll wonder why you couldn't have carried straight onwards and simply leave the forest to turn left. Either way, you emerge onto the open slopes of Two Rock Mountain. Walk gently uphill across this broad, boggy, grass and heather moorland, staying roughly parallel to a fence. After squelching across this slope, avoiding overtrodden parts around 450m, firmer footing is reached on an old embankment. Turn right to follow an obvious path downhill on top of the embankment. Turn left at the corner of a forest and continue downhill. The path stays close to the forest fence, then it leads through a thicket of gorse bushes next to a stand of trees and suddenly drops onto the R116 road at the head of Glencullen.

Turn left to follow the R116 road through Glencullen, passing the Pine Forest Arts Centre and a handful of small farms. A number of fields below the road are green and grassy, but the land above the road is generally uncultivated. You may spot a sign for Fox's, which claims to be the highest pub in Ireland, but the Wicklow Way turns right before the pub and follows a narrow road downhill to cross Glencullen River via Boranaraltry Bridge. If you need any food or drink, however, you'd be advised to detour into Glencullen village.

After crossing Boranaraltry Bridge, follow the road straight onwards and continue into a clear-felled stand of forest. Turn right to zig-zag uphill, then turn left along another forest track. A gradual ascent leads eventually to the edge of the forest and out onto the broad moorland slopes of Glencullen Mountain, or Prince William's

Powerscourt Waterfall seen from Ride Rock on the Wicklow Way

Walkers descend into Glenmalure with Mullacor rising beyond (Day 4)

Looking back to Lugnaquillia from the slopes of Shielstown Hill (Day 5)

Seat. You cross from Co Dublin into Co Wicklow and the Wicklow Way leads across a badly overtrodden bog where you should use boulders as stepping stones.

Forge onwards and follow a path back into the trees at Curtlestown Wood. The upper part of the path is very messy and you should be careful not to slip or trip on tree roots. The path leads onto a forest track, and this zig-zags down to land on a minor road. Turn right along this road, then turn left along another narrower road. There are fine views towards the head of Glencree, rising towards the great heathery bulk of Kippure - the highest point in Co Dublin at 757m. Its summit TV mast makes it a prominent landmark.

Turn left off the minor road to enter another forest and follow the forest track uphill across the slopes of Knockree. As the track contours around a clear-felled slope, there are fine views ahead of the Great Sugar Loaf. This is a landmark which can be seen from the northern part of the Wicklow Way and its classical, conical mountain profile makes it instantly recognisable. Other heights in the Wicklow Mountains tend to be broad-shouldered and more rounded. Look out for a sudden descent on the right, where a path picks a way down to a minor road only a short walk away from the whitewashed buildings of Knockree Youth Hostel.

Be warned in advance that you need to bring all your food supplies to Knockree Youth Hostel. The nearest shops, and for that matter alternative accommodation, are found 3 miles (5km) off-route at Enniskerry. Legions of walkers have arrived at the hostel without food and have had to make the long trek into town. The Youth Hostel occupies former farm buildings and has a splendid view across to the Great Sugar Loaf.

Marlay Park
Marlay House was rebuilt in the 19th century, while its stables and courtyard now houses interesting craft workshops and a small restaurant. The park grounds are well used by Dubliners and contain sports grounds, small wooded areas and ornamental gardens. Sculptures have been erected at many points in recent years - many of them of a strikingly modern design. There is also an orienteering course and fitness trail for the more energetic visitor. Dublin Bus number 47B serves the park.

**The Wicklow Way above Knockree and the shapely peak
of the Sugarloaf**

The Highest Pub in Ireland
Fox's Bar at Glencullen village claims to be the highest pub in Ireland - but then so does the Top of Coom near the edge of Co Kerry above Kilgarvan. Readers are encouraged to conduct their own researches, either by poring over detailed maps on dark, rainy nights, or more preferably, by making actual site visits and enjoying walks based on each of the pubs in question! Dublin Bus number 44B serves Glencullen - so there's no need to drink and drive.

DAY 3:
Knockree to Laragh
(Sketch map 2)

Distance: 18 miles (29km).

Maps: OS 1:50,000 Sheet 56.
OS 1:63,360 Map of Wicklow District.
OS 1:126,720 Sheet 16.

Leave Knockree Youth Hostel, turn right along the road and follow a track down through a forest before dropping straight down to Glencree River. You'll find a wooden footbridge which will spare you having to wade across the river. After crossing the footbridge, walk straight uphill to reach a forest track, then turn right to follow it. A left turn after a short while leads onto a minor road, where another left turn is required. Follow the minor road a short way to Crone, then turn right to enter a forest car park.

A forest track leads uphill from the car park and picnic area. Turn left onto another forest track, which cuts across a clear-felled slope. Another left turn leads along a track which climbs towards the edge of the forest at Ride Rock. A sudden view from the top of a steep slope takes in the Powerscourt Deerpark, Powerscourt Waterfall, the shapely peak of the Great Sugar Loaf and the broad moorland slopes of Djouce Mountain. After admiring this splendid

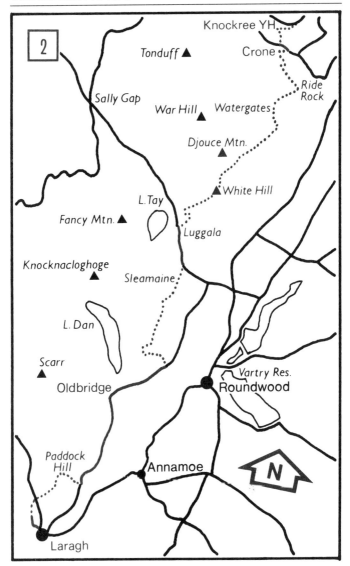

and varied scene, turn right and follow a path across the steep, wooded slope. There is one particularly rocky part along the way, then you can admire the prospect one last time before plunging into the depths of the forest.

The path has some messy patches, where you should be careful not to slip on tree roots, or trip over boulders. The path leads towards the edge of the forest and crosses the forest fence.

Djouce Mountain seems to fill the sky as you walk downhill alongside the forest fence. The River Dargle is spanned by a footbridge at the Watergates, then the Wicklow Way climbs uphill parallel to the edge of the forest. A ruined wall leads up to a heathery shoulder of Djouce Mountain, where a right turn takes the Wicklow Way away from the forest. The path seems to head straight towards the shapely summit of Djouce Mountain from time to time, and as you climb across its slopes you can debate whether or not to include the 725m summit in the Coast to Coast Walk. A path leads all the way to the summit trig point and the prospect of a fine view on a clear day, but the Wicklow Way actually bears off to the left and runs instead towards the lesser moorland hump of White Hill at 630m. A line of waymark posts show the course of the route, though these are rather sparse when you are trying to navigate across the slopes in mist.

Views from the open slopes of these hills take in a good stretch of the Wicklow coastline and on days of exceptional clarity you could see the distant summits of Snowdonia in North Wales. On the other side, views lead into the broad, bleak, boggy heart of the Wicklow wilderness. Kippure, Mullaghcleevaun, Tonelagee and lofty Lugnaquillia are arranged along the central axis of the Wicklow Mountains and are all being brought into the new Wicklow Mountains National Park.

Walk down from the crest of White Hill and cross a fence which crosses a rather boggy area near some forestry. After climbing over a slight rise there is a superb view over Lough Tay to the rugged face of Fancy Mountain, as well as along the length of the glen to Lough Dan and to points much further afield. The Wicklow Way passes a large boulder under which is a stone to the memory of J.B. Malone - "The Pioneer of the Wicklow Way". You may wish to pause and reflect for a moment that it was largely through this man's inspiration that you are now able to follow a waymarked trail from Coast to Coast across Ireland.

Continue down the path to reach a forest, where you turn left once and right twice to follow tracks which lead onto the R759 road at Luggala. Turn left to follow the road over a rise, then go down the road as if bound for the distant village of Roundwood. The road runs downhill with a forest on the left and a heathery slope on the right. You pass the Pier Gates and another track running off to the right, before a track leads off to the right into a forest at Sleamaine. This track rises and falls, emerging briefly from the trees to pass a small pool on a moorland gap. Continue along the track, passing across the top of a more cultivated slope, then keep an eye open for a path leaving the track on the right. This path passes along a forest ride to land down on another track, where you turn left. At the next junction, turn left again, then right. The track leads out of the forest at a farm and passes Forest Way Lodge.

Forest Way Lodge is a B&B which is conveniently located alongside the Wicklow Way and allows walkers to break this long day without the need to move off-route to Roundwood village for the night. If you wish to continue towards Glendalough, however, then you should follow the farm access road downhill and turn right along a minor road. The Wicklow Way leads straight through the next crossroads and runs down through woodlands to reach the Old Bridge near Lough Dan. Turn left after crossing the bridge and follow the road as it rises and falls, rises and falls again, crossing the shallow valleys and spurs far below the summit of Scarr. A Wicklow Way sign eventually points to a path entering a forest on the right. Follow this path uphill just inside the forest, then turn right along a forest track. Almost immediately, turn left to take a path slanting uphill roughly parallel to a more obvious forest track. This leads to a higher track, which you cross to pick up a path climbing more steeply uphill. This path emerges from the forest close to the summit of Paddock Hill.

Turn left on leaving the forest and walk downhill alongside the edge of the forest. Later, as indicated by a waymark, swing off to the right and walk down a brackeny slope to enter another forest. A track on the right runs down to the R115 road in Glenmacnass. Turn left to follow the road only a short way, then turn right to leave it by

Admiring Lough Tay and Fancy Mountain in the Wicklow wilderness

following a path across a clear-felled area to reach the Glenmacnass River. Cross a footbridge over the river and climb uphill to cross a forest track. The path leads to a farm access road, where a left turn leads down to St Kevin's Church. Another left turn along another road leads quickly down into the village of Laragh. A full range of services can be found right on the course of the Wicklow Way at this point - and you should note that it may be some time before you reach another point where you can stock up on supplies.

Powerscourt

The 18th century mansion of Powerscourt House and its ornamental gardens are well off the course of the Wicklow Way. The Powerscourt Deerpark, however, can be viewed from the lofty stance of the Ride Rock. The main scenic attraction is Powerscourt Waterfall, which slides down slabs of rock and is best observed after heavy rain. There are also delightful woodlands, which were mostly planted on bare ground earlier this century. The deerpark is now defunct, but you may catch glimpses of the descendants of former inhabitants - red deer, sika deer and red/sika hybrids. The dereliction of the former deer fence means that you may sight specimens far away from their original enclosure and you should keep an eye peeled for deer all the way along the Wicklow Way, if not further afield.

The Wicklow Mountains National Park

This national park has been established in a piecemeal fashion as various tracts of wilderness were acquired and managed by the Office of Public Works. Powerscourt and Glendalough formed the core areas of the new park and these places had long been on the tourist beat. When finally completed, the area of the national park should include the whole of the bleak and boggy axis of the Wicklow Mountains, stretching from Kippure to Lugnaquillia. A controversial interpretative centre was planned to occupy a forested site at Luggala, and indeed, the place is even marked on some maps of the Wicklow Mountains, but the development was halted after a protracted legal wrangle. The Office of Public Works has now to observe planning procedures and obtain planning permission for any future developments.

Roundwood

Roundwood is about 1 mile (1^1/$_2$km) off-route if you leave the Wicklow Way beyond Forest Way Lodge. The village offers a small range of shops, pubs and lodgings. There is also a campsite nearby - and there are very few of those along the entire Coast to Coast Walk. The village also claims to be the highest village in Ireland and stands at around 230m. The large Vartry Reservoir is just outside the village. St Kevin's Bus links Roundwood with Dublin and Glendalough.

Laragh

Laragh is the final gateway to Glendalough and this little village offers a good range of shops, pubs, tearooms and lodgings.

The Wicklow Way passes straight through the centre of the village and this is actually the only place on the course of the route which has such a splendid range of facilities. You should bear this in mind before leaving, as you may need to carry various food supplies away with you. There is an independent hostel in Laragh, another one on the Wicklow Way just outside the village, while

walkers intending to use the Youth Hostel should remain on the
Wicklow Way and pass through the ruins near the Round Tower to
reach the place. St Kevin's Bus offers a daily service to and from
Dublin.

DAY 4:
Laragh to Aughavannagh
(Sketch map 3)

Distance: 18 miles (29km).
Maps: OS 1:50,000 Sheets 56 and 62.
OS 1:63,360 Map of Wicklow District.
OS 1:126,720 Sheet 16.

Follow the R755 road, the Military Road, out of Laragh as if bound
for Glenmalure, but turn right to cross the Glendassan River, then
turn right again to pass through the courtyard of the Old Mill. This
is an independant hostel with a craft shop. A wooded track leads
straight onwards, running roughly parallel to the river, but keeping
largely out of sight of it. There is a sign inviting you to visit the ruins
of St Saviour's Priory - one of the famous Seven Churches. Later,
you can see the Glendalough Visitor Centre across the river, as well
as the strange structure known as St Kevin's Kitchen, the ruined
Cathederal and Round Tower. All these features are just off-route,
but you are recommended to cross the footbridge to explore them
all thoroughly. If you are keeping a tally, then remember that you
are looking for seven ruined churches in all around this former rural
monastic site.

The Wicklow Way continues along the wooded track, passing
the Lower Lake and almost reaching the Upper Lake. There is a
small information office, as well as waymarked nature trails in the
area, and of course more ruins and ancient stone crosses. The
Wicklow Way is routed up alongside the lovely Pollanass Waterfall,
following a path steeply uphill to join a forest track. Keep left on this

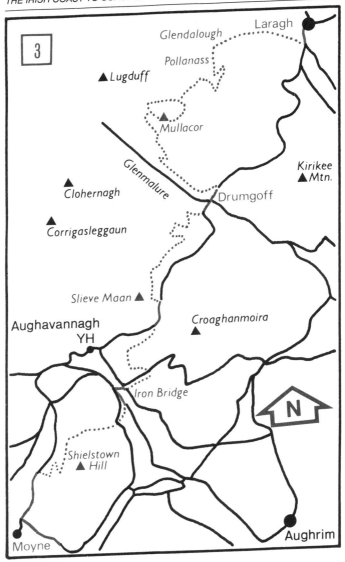

track to cross a bridge over Lugduff Brook, then climb further uphill.

Turn sharply right at the next junction of forest tracks (though you could continue straight on a short way for a superb view towards the head of Glendalough first). The track climbs up through the forest and bears right to cross a stream. Keep right in a clear-felled area to cross another stream, then turn left to follow the next track uphill roughly parallel to the stream. When you meet another forest track heading off to the right, you have a choice of routes - either over or around the summit of Mullacor.

If you follow the track straight onwards, then keep to the left, you'll emerge on a boggy gap at over 550m. However, there is also a path climbing steeply uphill from the track which, although rather boggy in places, emerges from the trees and climbs onto the boggy, grassy summit of Mullacor at 657m. This latter option is perhaps not recommended in wet and misty weather for dodgy navigators as it is rather sparsely waymarked. It is the highest point gained on the Wicklow Way, and indeed the entire Coast to Coast Walk, unless you have taken advantage of a climb up onto Djouce Mountain earlier in the walk. Anyone climbing Mullacor will need to descend north-west to reach the boggy gap at 550m.

Markers lead off the gap and down into Glenmalure. Follow these across the slopes of Mullacor to enter a forest. A path leads down a forest ride onto a forest track, where you turn left to continue walking downhill. As you descend, take the next track on the right, then left, then right again. You should now be walking as if towards the head of Glenmalure, but look out for a path on the left which leads down to a lower track, where you turn left again. You should now find yourself walking towards the foot of Glenmalure. The slopes have been clear-felled, so as you climb gradually along the track you can enjoy splendid views of the rugged surroundings. The mountainside rising on the opposite side of the glen is Clohernagh, which provides a route to the lofty summit of Lugnaquillia - the highest mountain in both Co Wicklow and the Province of Leinster at 925m. Although apparently shapeless, Lugnaquillia can often be recognised in more distant views simply by its sheer bulk.

The forest track climbs gently and contours around the side of

Glenmalure before swinging leftwards and descending. Make a right turn onto another track, which in turn leads down to a minor road by a bridge. This is the Military Road, which is followed through the next crossroads. First, though, you may wish to break at the Glenmalure Lodge, which offers food, drink and lodgings to weary wayfarers. It is the only place offering such facilities for a considerable distance, so think twice before moving onwards.

When you follow the Military Road across Drumgoff Bridge, note the large ruined barracks on the left, then leave the road by following a forest track on the right. This climbs up the slope, then you need to turn left and continue uphill. At the next junction, turn right and zig-zag uphill. Next, take two left turns and cross a stream in a high, shallow valley. After passing a small hut, turn right up a path which climbs across a clear-felled slope. The path crosses other tracks, then it suddenly turns left to join a track. Turn right to follow this forest track uphill and across the slopes of Slieve Maan. Continue along it until, on the left, a forest ride runs downhill and frames the shapely peak of Croaghanmoira.

Follow the ride downhill, then climb a short way towards the Military Road. Turn right to walk parallel to the road until a stile gives access to it. Follow the road into the forest, then take a track off to the left. This rises through the forest and continues as a path around the slopes of Carrickashane Mountain. Bear right to follow another track downhill and keep right along the next track to descend onto a rather patchy minor road. Turn right to walk down this road, then look out for a track on the left which completes the descent into the valley, reaching another minor road near the Iron Bridge which spans the Ow River. Don't cross the bridge yet, but turn off-route and follow the road towards the tiny village of Aughavannagh. Turn left to reach the youth hostel, which is in an old barracks building hidden behind a screen of tall trees.

There is no other accommodation anywhere near Aughavannagh, nor is there a shop closer than Askanagap, so you should remember to carry in all your food supplies. It's also a good idea to check well in advance that there is a bed waiting for you in this remote place.

Round Tower rising above the rural monastic site at Glendalough

45

Glendalough

Glendalough is where St Kevin lived as a hermit and inhabited a cave known as St Kevin's Bed high above the Upper Lake. To mortify his flesh, he waded into the cold waters of the lake and raised his hands in prayer. So fervently did he pray that he didn't notice a bird building a nest in his outstretched palm. Being a gentle man, he waited until the eggs were hatched and the fledglings flown before leaving the lake. Of such men are legends born! Glendalough duly became a centre of pilgrimage and a rural monastic site became a notable centre of learning. Start your explorations at the Glendalough Visitor Centre, where an audio-visual display will give you some of the background to the area. The ruins of the Seven Churches, Round Tower and Cathedral can all be explored with the aid of a small map/guide. The Round Tower is a perfect example of such structures, with its narrow doorway high above the ground, small windows around the top, with a conical top finishing off the tower. Rural monasticism grew from the 6th century, but later Norman influences replaced this type of site with much larger cathedrals and monasteries - which in turn generally fell ruinous after the Dissolution. Pilgrimages to Glendalough in later times were marred by faction fighting and riots until the event became so unruly that it had to be banned altogether. Up to that time, by some curious reckoning, seven pilgrimages to Glendalough were deemed to carry the same merit as one pilgrimage to Rome!

The Military Road

For many centuries the Wicklow Mountains were well beyond the Pale and English influence from Dublin held little sway over the area. The O'Byrnes held the glens for their own and were able to repel any forces which were sent into the mountains. In 1580 an English force was despatched to Glenmalure and roundly defeated, with Edmund Spenser and Walter Raleigh being among those fleeing for their lives! It was the 1798 Rebellion which finally brought changes into the Wicklow Mountains, as the English forces were once again at a distinct disadvantage in this terrain, and took steps to tame the wilderness once and for all. Soldiers and navvies laboured over the mountains from Dublin in the early 1800s laying a military road over the bogs and around mountainsides to penetrate

Aughavannagh Youth Hostel occupies a former British Army barracks

the remotest glens. To house the soldiers, a series of barracks were constructed at strategic points, such as Glencree, Laragh, Glenmalure and Aughavannagh. However, the construction of the road and barracks took a considerable time and by the end of it all the rebels of the 98 were mostly dead and buried. The Glencree barracks later served as a Reformatory and again as a centre for Christian Reconciliation, but currently lie derelict. The barracks at Laragh were ultimately demolished and the stonework used throughout the village. The Drumgoff barracks in Glenmalure are in ruins, though remain as a substantial edifice. At Aughavannagh, the barracks were used as a hunting lodge by Charles Stewart Parnell - "The Uncrowned King of Ireland" - but now offer basic accommodation in this remote place for Youth Hostellers. The Military Road is now fully signposted as a scenic and historic drive through the mountains and it offers splendid access to a whole range of superb mountain walks.

DAY 5:
Aughavannagh to Tinahely
(Sketch maps 3-4)

Distance: 14 miles (22km).

Maps: OS 1:50,000 Sheet 62.
           OS 1:126,720 Sheets 16 and 19.

Leave Aughavannagh and return to the Iron Bridge, and this time you can cross over the Ow River. Pause before turning left along the next road to admire the bulky form of Lugnaquillia, then follow the road through the valley. A forest track on the right climbs up to a slightly higher road, where you turn left and almost immediately cross a bridge over a stream. Turn right to follow a forest track up a clear-felled slope. The track stays fairly close to the stream and passes through a crossroads of forest tracks before crossing over a forested gap. On the descent, there may be a fine view ahead of Mount Leinster - which will be reached in the next couple of days of walking.

After crossing the forested gap, look out for another forest track which descends to the right. Follow this downhill through a clear-felled area and turn left along another forest track. This later bends to the right and runs down to a minor road. Turn left along this road and walk past pleasant farmlands. There are two roads off to the right, but don't follow them. The first one crosses a river and the second one reaches the tiny village of Moyne. There is nothing to draw walkers into Moyne, so stay on the road above the village and follow it uphill a short way. Watch out for a turning on the right, where a delightfully grassy track descends to another minor road near a holy well. Turn left along the lower road, then right to follow another road down to Sandyford Bridge. Look into the water flowing beneath the bridge and you will appreciate that this was once indeed a sandy ford. As you climb above the bridge, be sure to turn left along a muddy, stony road and not the forest track which runs above it. The road runs through a most pleasant valley with forested slopes rising above a strip of green fields. The patchy road climbs uphill past farms and reaches an old school which has been converted into a house. Branch left at this point to follow the road back down into the valley.

You'll reach a bridge over a river, but don't cross over it. Instead, look for a turning on the right which leads immediately across a ford. This is a vigorous waterway and after a spell of rain you can expect to get wet feet at this point. An old trackway runs uphill through a handful of rickety gates, before it forges across the more open slopes of Garryhoe Mountain. Views from the hillside are charming and extend across a patchwork landscape of fields and small woodlands, with range upon rolling range of little hills crowding the scene. You should also look out for a prominent circular rath (earth fort) on the upper slope of the hillside, if you find yourself fording a small stream, then you've already gone past it.

A track on the left runs down to a farmhouse B&B, but to continue the walk you should bear right and pass the Doctor's Cross. This is a small monument to a doctor who was killed in a shooting accident. If you find yourself running short of time, then another track on the left could be used to make a rapid descent to Tinahely. The Wicklow Way, however, keeps right and heads towards a woodland.

Follow this track into the woods and keep left to pass an old farmstead. Turn right when the track leaves the woods at a junction with another track. The Wicklow Way continues along a track which contours around the lower slopes of Coolafunshoge Mountain. As you open and close the gates along this track, you may feel that you're drifting further and further away from Tinahely, but at length a sudden turning to the left reveals a road which runs down to ford the Derry River. There is a footbridge just beside the ford, then you simply turn left along the R747 road and follow this straight into Tinahely. There are roadside B&Bs, with Murphy's Hotel actually in the centre of town, along with a small range of shops and pubs.

Shielstown Hill

There is an avalanche disaster story connected with Shielstown Hill, which has given this otherwise unremarkable height a measure

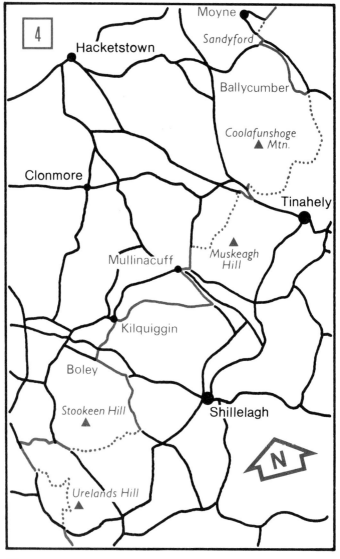

Walking on a delightful track round the slopes of Garryhoe Mountain

of notoriety. It was in the 1860s and a considerable depth of snow on the southern face suddenly slumped. Some say it all started with a snowball fight, but however it happened, an entire family in a cottage on the hillside was wiped out. This is apparently the only case of avalanche deaths ever recorded in Ireland.

Tinahely
This fine little Georgian town has three roads branching from a central triangular area. A fully range of facilities is available for tired, hungry and thirsty wayfarers. The general air is quiet, but there is a horse fair and agricultural show each August. Bus Eireann table number 58 serves Tinahely on Thursdays and Sundays only, offering links with Dublin and Wexford.

> # DAY 6:
> # *Tinahely to Clonegal*
> ## *(Sketch maps 4-5)*

Distance:	18 miles (29km).
Maps:	OS 1:50,000 Sheet 62.
	OS 1:126,720 Sheet 19.

Tinahely is a little off the Wicklow Way, so steps need to be retraced along the R747 road to Glenphilipeen, where a minor road heads off up to the left. At the top of this road, turn left again, but don't go along the farm access road. Instead, make sure that you are following an old trackway further to the left which leads to a gate. Turn left yet again at this gate, then bear right to follow an old track in a gorse-lined hollow around the foot of Muskeagh Hill. There are a few rickety gates along the way. When the track descends near a farm, turn left to walk alongside a forest, then turn right to walk down to a minor road. Turn left to follow this road onwards.

You should note that a considerable stretch of road-walking now follows. Make a right turn at the next junction and take the road across a river to reach the tiny crossroads village of Mullinacuff. Take the second road off to the left here and follow it gradually uphill to Stranakelly Crossroads, where a small pub offers a place to break for a while. Facilities are extremely limited on this day's walk, unless you head off-route to Shillelagh. Turn right at the pub and climb more steeply uphill from the crossroads. The road leads across the slopes of Cronelea, then descends to Kilquiggin Crossroads. Turn left here and pass St Finian's Church and school. Head through the next staggered crossroads and walk up to Boley. Turn left and follow the road over a rise, then look out for a road on the right which runs down to cross a stream. Follow this road steeply uphill from the bridge and climb alongside the edge of Raheenakitt Forest, which has been planted on Stookeen Hill.

Once the top of the road is reached, a forest track runs off to the right. Follow this, then turn right again to climb uphill. After the next right turn, continue straight onwards to exit from the forest into a high field which will be seen through a gap in the trees. A muddy trackway, deeply rutted in places, descends through the field, then there is a very muddy farmyard which you may have to wade through before a firmer footing is reached on the continuing track. Follow this next track further downhill to reach a minor road. Turn right to follow the road downhill, then turn left to walk further downhill to cross a stream. The road begins to twist and turn as it climbs, but a left turn leads along a straighter road for a while.

A left turn off the road leads along a track on the forested slopes of Moylisha Hill. Turn right along another track, then right again at a small hut. Almost immediately, a left turn along another track leads uphill, and you should keep left at the next junction too. A sharp right turn onto another track leads across the upper slopes of Urelands Hill, offering a splendid view of the bulky form of Mount Leinster - easily distinguished by its summit TV mast. Make another sharp right turn to descend from Urelands Hill, then turn left to leave the forest. When you hit a minor road, turn left, then almost immediately right to follow another road signposted for Clonegal. This road runs downhill, then a right turn leads across Wicklow Bridge. You cross from Co Wicklow into Co Carlow at this point and the road continues towards the village of Clonegal. There is nearby accommodation in Clonegal, but no bus service. A Wicklow Way mapboard is mounted just off a green and you can study the course of the Wicklow Way one last time before the Coast to Coast Walk continues onto the South Leinster Way. Food and drink are obtainable from a couple of shops and pubs.

Shillelagh
Although Sillelagh is off the course of the Wicklow Way, some wayfarers do in fact go there in search of food or lodgings. Just outside of the little town are the remains of the Coolattin oakwoods - a mere remnant of the once extensive oakwoods which once clothed lowland Co Wicklow. The great oaks were cut since the Normans arrived to make roof beams for such notable places as Westminster Hall, while particularly straight trunks would have been taken for ship's masts. The decimation of the oakwoods has

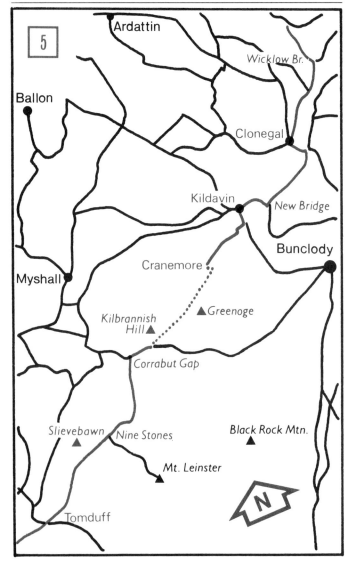

only just been stopped after one final assault and now it is to be hoped that some conservation work and replanting will take place.

Clonegal

When the Wicklow Way was being planned, it was originally intended that the route would terminate at the tiny village of Moyne. At that time, however, a whole network of trails was being planned throughout Ireland and one of these was the South Leinster Way. A decision was made to extend the Wicklow Way southwards to Clonegal, so that an easy link could be made with the South Leinster Way, which itself starts down the road in the village of Kildavin. For a hero's welcome at the end of the Wicklow Way, you should aim to stay at Park Lodge Farm some distance outside of Clonegal.

THE SOUTH LEINSTER WAY

DAY 7:
Clonegal to Borris
(Sketch maps 5-6)

Distance: 17 miles (27km).
Maps: OS 1:50,000 Sheet 68 (not yet published).
             OS 1:126,720 Sheet 19.

There are no waymarks between Clonegal, at the end of the Wicklow Way, and Kildavin, at the start of the South Leinster Way. However, an easy link can be made between the two trails by walking along minor roads. You should leave Clonegal by following the road across Derry River to reach Watch House Village on the opposite bank. Turn right along another road, which climbs above and away from the river for a while, but drops down to it again as a right turn is made across the New Bridge. The road continues to Kildavin - a little village by-passed by the main N80 road. There is a shop and a pub, while across the road a South Leinster Way mapboard can be inspected.

Turn left after looking at the mapboard and follow the road uphill as if going to Bunclody. Cross the main road and continue along Ballypierce Lane, which runs gradually uphill and has a sudden left and right turn on it. You follow the road past farms as if heading to the upper part of the valley at Cranemore, but keep an eye open for a forest track rising on the left from the road. The track rises up the hillside and bears left, then swings to the right and runs across the slopes of Greenoge. There are some unplanted and clear-felled slopes along the way, where views stretch back towards the distant Wicklow Mountains.

The track climbs gradually across the slope, then almost imperceptibly it crosses a shallow gap between the heights of

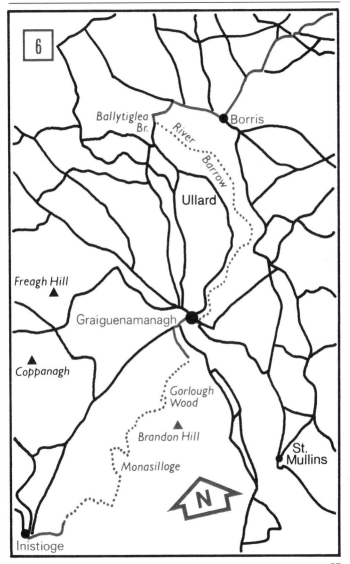

Greenoge and Kilbrannish Hill. A gradual descent from a left turn leads to a road, where you turn right and walk uphill. The road leads to the Corrabut Gap at around 350m, where a left turn leads along the Mount Leinster Drive. This scenic road rises from a forest and cuts across the rugged, heathery slopes of Mount Leinster to reach the Nine Stones on a gap at around 450m. The Nine Stones are small upright blocks of stone arranged in a line just to the side of the road.

The road passes between Slievebawn at 525m and Mount Leinster at 792m. The latter mountain can be ascended by following a road to the summit TV mast - an optional detour from the South Leinster Way on a clear day as there is an exceptionally wide-ranging view. Mount Leinster is the highest mountain in both Co Carlow and Co Wexford and from its summit you could look back to the Wicklow Mountains, across the patchwork central plains, and away to the distant Galty Mountains and neighbouring ranges, which will take some days to reach.

To continue the walk from the Nine Stones, however, the road is followed down across the rugged slopes of Slievebawn. You will notice blocks of quartz-rich rock scattered across the hillside, while far below in the valley you may spot Mount Leinster House in a gap between the trees. The South Leinster Way goes through two crossroads in quick succession at Tomduff, then continues across the slopes of Knockgaur. Turn right at the next road junction, then left, then quickly right again. Follow the road onwards, avoiding a right turn, but turning right at the next crossroads. The road crosses a small bridge, then heads straight towards Borris and offers fine views along the rugged, bouldery flanks of the Blackstairs Mountains. The road passes beneath an old railway viaduct, then turns right to climb up through the village of Borris, which offers a small range of facilities for passing wayfarers.

Borris

Borris is obviously an estate village, with all the main buildings on one side of the road and a tall boundary wall opposite which is punctuated by a couple of gateways. Borris House is out of sight in the wooded demesne beyond the wall, but it is the ancestral seat of the MacMurrough Kavanaghs - a family descended from the kings of Leinster. With an illustrious history behind them, the family has several remarkable members. Art was poisoned in 1417 and his funeral cortege filled the road for 6 miles (10km) from New Ross to St Mullins. Morgan was a giant of a man who for a time served with the king of Prussia. The king was reluctant to let him go home, but Morgan said that he would bring his brothers back, whom he claimed were even bigger men! The king reluctantly let him go, and never saw him again. Arthur was born in 1831 with neither arms nor legs, yet he became an accomplished rider, hunter and Member of Parliament, as well as a world traveller. Borris offers limited accommodation, and a few shops and pubs. If you decide to go for an evening stroll, you could walk across the old railway viaduct. There is no bus service.

DAY 8:
Borris to Inistioge
(Sketch map 6)

Distance: 18 miles (29km).

Maps: OS 1:50,000 Sheet 68 (not yet published).
OS 1:126,720 Sheet 19.

Follow the R702 road uphill to leave the village of Borris - or alternatively you could walk along a very narrow strip of land sandwiched between the road and the boundary wall of Borris House. As the road leaves the village, look out for another road on the left which is signposted for Graiguenamanagh. This leads down to Ballytiglea Bridge which spans the River Barrow. Don't cross the bridge, but turn left to gain the towpath of the river and continue downstream along it.

Both the South Leinster Way and the Barrow Way are routed along the towpath to Graiguenamanagh. Woodlands flank the towpath and a side-channel leads to Borris Lock. Beyond the lock, the towpath follows the natural course of the river again and crosses the inflowing Mountain River, which comes down from the

Blackstairs Mountains and passes by Borris. Another side-channel leads to Ballingrane Lock, then the towpath continues further downstream.

Clashganna Lock is reached next, situated at the foot of a steep, wooded slope. Anyone with time to spare could follow a road uphill from the lock-house, bearing to the right to find a small roadside car park which offers a splendid aerial view of the lock. The South Leinster Way, however, stays low on the towpath and proceeds downstream from Clashganna, following a lengthy side-channel towards Ballykennan Lock. This is actually a double lock, so it takes twice as long for boats to negotiate it compared to previous locks. The remaining stretch of the River Barrow flowing to Graiguenamanagh has no locks. Simply follow the towpath between the broad river and the steep, wooded, rocky slope above it. There are some broad bends to walk around before the bulk of Brandon Hill comes into view and the town of Graiguenamanagh appears. Note the Cornmill Lodge across the river - a hotel converted from an old mill on the quayside. Beyond is the roof of the abbey church - also restored from a ruinous state. You cross over an old arched bridge to enter town, and also cross from Co Carlow to Co Kilkenny in the process. The narrow main street is filled with shops and pubs and there is accommodation also available if required.

To continue along the South Leinster Way, turn left onto the New Ross road and follow it uphill, then turn right along a minor road for Inistioge. As you climb up this road, with fine views back towards Mount Leinster and the Blackstairs Mountains, turn left along a farm access road. This is signposted as the South Leinster Way, but you will also notice a stone tablet marked with the capitals BW - which stands for Brandon Way. Both routes follow the access road at first, passing a farm on a gravel track, then keeping right to enter a forest. At the next junction of tracks, however, the Brandon Way goes off to the left (the stone tablet is marked with the word GO), but the South Leinster Way goes straight onwards (and passes a Brandon Way marker bearing the word RETURN). Follow the forest track to another junction of tracks, where you turn left and zig-zag steeply uphill. Take the next track on the right (though you could zig-zag above the forest to climb to the 518m summit of Brandon Hill, which is the highest point in Co Kilkenny). The track runs through the forest and turns left to emerge onto an open slope offering good views across to the little hill of Coppanagh, then it goes back into the forest to emerge on another moorland slope.

A wide loop takes the track down a clear-felled slope. Go through a crossroads of tracks at the bottom, then turn left at the next junction. Climb gradually up this track until you reach the upper edge of the forest again. Turn right around the edge of the forest and follow a muddy track which runs parallel to an even muddier track. This later bends to the left and becomes very muddy and even completely waterlogged in places. However, this is the track which will lead you quickly through the upland pastures and down towards the valley of the River Nore. Simply keep to the most obvious track when you reach any junctions, and a narrow road will eventually lead past small farms to join another minor road above the River Nore. Turn right and follow the road towards Inistioge. When you reach another road junction, proceed straight down a short, steep road which is barred to traffic, then cross a fine, arched bridge to enter the village. A full, though limited range of facilities are available in this charming place, where olde worlde buildings surround a square green.

The River Barrow
The Barrow is the second longest river in Ireland after the mighty Shannon. It rises in the Slieve Bloom and flows southwards to reach the sea via Waterford Harbour. It is becoming more and more popular with pleasure cruisers and you may notice the familiar blue and white Celtic Canal Cruisers from Tullamore. The towpath of the river is available as a long distance walking route called the Barrow Way. In fact, an Act of Parliament of 1537 required that "seven feet of plaine ground" be reserved alongside the river as a towpath and access route. The Barrow Way links with the Grand Canal Way at Lowtown, so that an easy, low-level, continuous towpath walk links Dublin with Graiguenamanagh, or Graiguenamanagh with the River Shannon at Shannon Harbour in Co Offaly. The Barrow Way continues a little way southwards of Graiguenamanagh to the monastic site of St Mullins, so that the full length of the walk from Lowtown to St Mullins is 70 miles (113km).

Graiguenamanagh

The Cistercians founded Duiske Abbey by the River Barrow in 1204. After the Dissolution of the 16th century, the abbey decayed and became a useful quarry for building at least part of the town of Graiguenamanagh. In 1813 the original abbey church was re-roofed and other restoration works were carried out on the building. However, much of the original structure of the abbey has gone and its former extent is now buried beneath the narrow, winding streets of the town. Many of Graiguenamanagh's buildings have traditional frontages and lie cheek by jowl in a delightfully haphazard fashion. One of the most recent of the old buildings to be restored is the Cornmill Lodge down by the quayside. There are B&Bs around town, as well as a good range of shops and pubs. There used to be a river and canalboat service between Graiguenamanagh and Portobello in Dublin, but these days the only public transport is offered by Bus Eireann table number 56. This is a Saturday only service to Dublin and Kilkenny.

Brandon Hill

This bulky little hill rises above Graiguenamanagh and bears a summit cross of recent origin. It can be climbed from the South Leinster Way, while the circular Brandon Way is waymarked around it by stone plinths carrying tablets inscribed with the letters BW. Towards the end of the Coast to Coast Walk, you may catch a glimpse of its much taller namesake - Brandon Mountain on the Dingle Peninsula in Co Kerry. The hill used to be a renowned game reserve, and hence was popular with poachers too. An occurrence known as the "Brandon Shootings" recalls a scuffle between four gamekeepers and three poachers resulting in one death on either side. Walkers these days will have no such problems wandering over the heathery heights, though there are some exceptionally rugged slopes falling towards the River Barrow which are best avoided altogether.

Inistioge

This charming little village has a small range of shops, pubs and lodgings. There is a central square green which has been planted with trees and monuments, and this is flanked by a series of very interesting traditional frontages. These frontages have admittedly had some recent work done to them to create an appropriate outdoor setting for certain scenes which were filmed around Maeve Binchy's book *Good Girls*. The village originally grew around a small monastic site which had developed a small area of land alongside the River Nore and operated a salmon fishery. The only public transport is offered by Bus Eireann table number 71, which offers a Thursday only service between New Ross and Kilkenny.

DAY 9:
Inistioge to Mullinavat
(Sketch map 7)

Distance:	18 miles (29km).
Maps:	OS 1:50,000 Sheet 68 (not yet published) and 75.
	OS 1:126,720 Sheet 23.

Leave Inistioge's green by following a short road through a gateway, where a track running parallel to the River Nore offers a riverside walk. The River Nore is actually tidal at this point, so you might find the water flowing either way. However, the Coast to Coast Walk is nowhere near halfway completed despite the sea water reaching this rural backwater. There is a picnic table under a tree, where the village of Inistioge can be seen one last time before being lost to view. There is also a nearby memorial to four teenagers who died in a drowning tragedy, and flowers are often found next to it. Follow the track across a steep, wooded slope, passing a stout old ice-house which served the nearby Woodstock House. The house was burnt in the 1920s and now the estate is managed as a state forest.

The track crosses a clear-felled slope with fine views along the snaking course of the River Nore. Avoid any tracks which lead down towards the river, until you reach a cul-de-sac sign. Turn right at this point and start following the track up a gentle slope in sweeping zig-zags which lead to the top end of the forest. Watch for

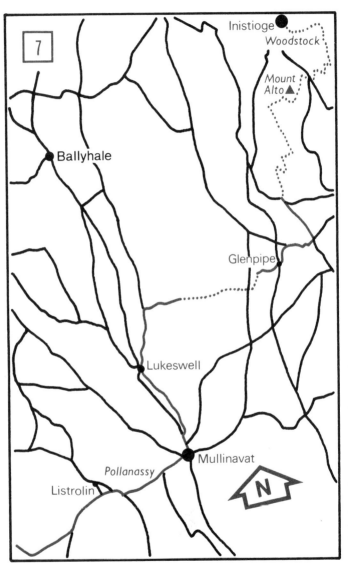

7

Inistioge
Woodstock
Mount Alto ▲
Ballyhale
Glenpipe
Lukeswell
Pollanassy
Listrolin
Mullinavat
N

Approaching Graiguenamanagh from the towpath of the River Barrow

Perched above Pollanassy Waterfall near the village of Mullinavat (Day 10)

Following the towpath of the River Suir away from Carrick on Suir (Day 11)

waymarks at junctions of tracks along the way, then when the track runs onto a minor road, turn right to pass a house at a road junction. Just beyond the junction, another forest track heads off uphill on the left. This track bears right, then left, as it climbs and there are views back across the valley of the River Nore to the hump of Brandon Hill and the rugged range of the Blackstairs Mountains.

The track passes around the forested summit of Mount Alto - a minor height with an ambitious name - then drops down the far slope and turns left to reach the edge of the forest. As you leave the forest, turn left again and follow an old track uphill passing a number of fields which are well removed from farms. This track climbs gradually, then you need to turn right along another grassy old track which is flanked with gorse bushes. This track stays close to the broad crest of the hill and passes more fields. Views westwards across the plains may feature the prominent hump of Slievenamon, as well as the Comeragh and Galty Mountains.

The track reaches the clear-felled corner of a forest, where you should turn right along a forest track. This track runs downhill past the remaining stands of trees, passing close to a few fields on the descent, then emerges onto a minor road near a farm. Turn left to walk up the road, then branch to the right at a fork in the road. This road rises gently, falls to cross a stream, then rises to a crossroads. Turn right at the crossroads and walk downhill to cross the Arrigle River. Glenpipe is reached - which is no more than a couple of farms together in the valley. Turn left to pass them and continue up a wet and muddy road and keep going up through a crossroads. Look out for a turning on the left as you proceed further uphill, where a track leads through a clear-felled forest. This forest track runs across a gentle slope and passes back into stands of trees. By bearing right along the most obvious track you'll be brought out onto a minor road near a tall mast.

Make a right turn along the road, then within a short distance turn left to follow a broad forest track. This runs over a forested rise and leads straight downhill to exit from the forest. Follow a minor road past a couple of farms, then later turn left along another road, which leads to the tiny village of Lukeswell, where facilities are limited to a single pub if you need a break. If you want to continue, then pass the pub on the main N9 road and turn left to walk up a much quieter, narrow minor road. This has a patchy surface at times, but is largely traffic-free, though running roughly parallel to the main road and railway line. Towards the end of this minor road you may spot a white cross at a road junction, which records a mission once held in the parish. The road leads downhill and passes under the railway to join the main N9 road again. Turn left and follow this busy road into the village of Mullinavat, which has shops, pubs and a small range of lodgings for the night.

The River Nore
The River Nore, along with the Barrow and Suir, flows towards the sea at Waterford Harbour. Collectively, the rivers are known as the "Three Sisters of Ireland". In ancient legend, all the great rivers of Ireland had their source at a single, sacred well. This magical well was called Connle's Well and was supposed to be somewhere in the Slieve Bloom. It began to flow on the night that Conn of the Hundred Battles was born. Hazels overhung the well and crimson nuts which fell from the branches were eaten by the Salmon of Knowledge... all of which should point towards the deep reverence shown towards wells and water in centuries gone by. These days, occasional cruisers will tackle the tidal reaches of the Nore and a mooring is available quite close to Inistioge, but this sort of cruising is generally reserved for experienced practitioners.

Woodstock
The Tighe family had their seat at Woodstock House and the most recent building dates from the 1740s. It was held to be one of the most magnificent houses in Ireland, but was burnt during the Troubles of the 1920s. There are still some features worth searching for, such as the ice-house which is passed by the South Leinster Way, while off-route can be found the Dovecote and terraced gardens. The estate is now managed as a state forest, but contains a variety of trees which were planted long before the commercial plantations.

Mullinavat
This is a long and straggly village, lying on the main N9 road and on the railway between Dublin and Waterford. The village has shops, pubs and limited accommodation, and although there is no

railway station, there are plenty of buses passing through. Bus Eireann table number 82 offers a daily service to points such as Dublin, Waterford and Dungarvan, while table number 70, which runs only on Thursdays, passes through Mullinavat on its way from Waterford to Thomastown.

DAY 10:
Mullinavat to Carrick on Suir
(Sketch maps 7-8)

Distance: 15 miles (24km).

Maps: OS 1:50,000 Sheet 75.
             OS 1:126,720 Sheets 22 and 23.

Today's stretch of the South Leinster Way is entirely along minor roads, bringing this portion of the Coast to Coast Walk as far as Carrick on Suir. Start by following the main N9 road through Mullinavat, then turn right along a minor road which crosses Black Water and goes straight onwards to cross the Pollanassa River. The road climbs uphill, then a sign on the right indicates a scenic waterfall at Pollanassy, which has access via a short gravel path leading downhill from the road. The detour to view the waterfall takes only a couple of minutes and it has long been a notable local attraction despite its small size. A picnic site is immediately adjacent.

Continue up the minor road, taking the next turning right, followed by a left turn. Signposts indicate Piltown, which will be reached in due course. Keep straight on at two junctions near Listrolin, then bear right at the next fork in the road to follow a road up past a small forest. Keep high on this road and pass through a crossroads at Tobernabrone. Farms and houses are passed, then you take a left fork downhill and keep left at the next junction. Follow the road straight downhill, then bear right to reach another junction of minor roads. Turn left and a straight road leads towards a junction of roads near an old gatehouse.

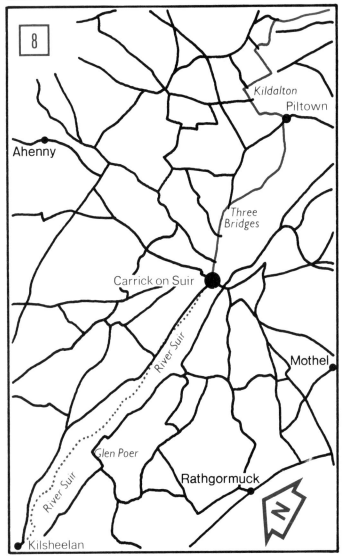

The gatehouse stands at the edge of the Kildalton College grounds, so turn right to follow the road onwards to Sandpits Cross Roads. A left turn at the crossroads leads onto the R698 road, which can be followed past the entrance gates of Kildalton College, and on into Piltown. This little village straddles the busy N24 road and has a couple of shops and pubs for walkers who want to take a break. You need to cross the busy main road and turn right along it for a short way, then turn left where a picnic table sits on a small green beside a bridge. A minor road at this point offers an alternative to a walk along the main road to Carrick on Suir. The minor road has a rather muddy surface in places, but is generally quiet and passes a few farms and houses - some of them derelict. You could make a slight detour to visit an old graveyard along the way, while later you will notice Tibberaghy Castle from the roadside - a tower house which is still inhabited.

The minor road eventually runs back towards the main N24 road. Turn right along the main road, then left to follow a minor road. This crosses the Lingaun River, taking you from Co Kilkenny into the South Riding of Co Tipperary. Turn right onto the main road later and aim for the centre of town, where a narrow street is lined with a good range of shops and pubs. The South Leinster Way ends here - and the Coast to Coast Walk continues along the Munster Way.

Carrick on Suir

This town was founded in the 13th century and originally bore the name of Carrickmagriffin. The River Suir is tidal up to the town and was in fact the main transport route to and from Carrick. Norman influence was for a time restricted largely to the riverside, which is evidenced by the number of tower houses along the way. There is accommodation in and around Carrick, plus a fine range of shops and pubs, along with a Tourist Information Office. There is a railway station, while Bus Eireann has a comprehensive listing of daily destinations and other services which can be checked with reference to table numbers 56, 66, 84, 105, 113, 146 and 213.

THE MUNSTER WAY

DAY 11:
Carrick on Suir to Clonmel
(Sketch maps 8-9)

Distance: 17 miles (27km).

Maps: 1:25,000 Comeragh Mountains Map (not an OS map).
            OS 1:50,000 Sheet 75.
            OS 1:126,720 Sheet 22.

The Munster Way runs from Carrick on Suir to the Vee Gap high in the Knockmealdown Mountains, taking the Coast to Coast Walk through its halfway point, which for practical reasons could be said to be Clonmel - on account of its excellent transport links. To reach the start of the Munster Way, you should walk down to the River Suir at Carrick on Suir, turn right and walk upstream. Just on the edge of town is a small car park in between the river and the main N24 road. A Munster Way mapboard can be studied, which is accompanied by a board full of angling information. You should study the angling maps too, as the fishing beats are the best trodden parts of the old towpath and the stretch in between, where fishing is restricted, can be rather more overgrown as it is used less often.

A good, firm riverside path leads away from the park on the edge of Carrick, passing the moorings of narrow, flat-bottomed fishing cots. The path continues onwards, sandwiched between a stout wall and the river, then a small car park is reached. As you continue upstream, the riverbanks become more vegetated, though you may notice that the path is actually built up from the river on blocks of stone. Also, look out for a curious little tower on the opposite bank of the river, which was built so that a salmon weir could be kept under close observation. The path is narrow and often surfaced with gravel, but there are a couple of muddy patches and eventually the gravel surface peters out.

After passing another point where cars have access to the riverbank, the path can become more thickly vegetated in summer. Obviously, more walkers are required along that stretch to keep the undergrowth trodden back! Unfortunately, the path seems to rely largely on the boots of fishermen, and so the stretch where fishing is restricted has only a poorly trodden path. Nor does it have the occasional little benches or shelter huts of the earlier part of the walk. You may notice the ruins of Glen Castle across the river, or a small ruined chapel on a rise on the same side as you are walking. The path becomes better as you approach Kilsheelan and the next fishing beat. Another tower house will be noticed ahead, and at that point there is a turbulent bend in the River Suir where the banks have had to be buttressed with stone for protection. After rounding that bend you will reach Kilsheelan Bridge, where you turn right to climb up to the road from the side of the bridge.

If you need food, drink or accommodation, then you can turn right and walk into Kilsheelan village on the main N24 road. There are also frequent buses. If you want to continue along the Munster Way, however, then turn left to cross Kilsheelan Bridge and follow the road to a junction where there is a monument to Count Le Poer. Bear left at this point, then cross the road to enter a forest at a roadside lodge. A forest track climbs uphill and you keep left at first in Kilsheelan Woods, then take the track to the right at the next junction to start climbing in sweeping zig-zags. As you climb up a clear-felled slope, take the next track off to the left, then climb uphill admiring views away across the River Suir to the shapely form of Slievenamon. The Munster Way takes a track on the right back into the trees and it climbs gradually across the slopes of Carricktober in a fairly straight line.

Take no notice of other tracks branching off to the left or right, but keep climbing along the track until a slight descent leads past the prominent standing stone of Cloghfadda. You might also have a view from time to time of the sharp Knockanaffrin ridge high in the Comeragh Mountains. The track reaches the edge of the forest and continues through a field to reach a minor road near Harney's Cross Roads. You could head straight onwards to reach an independent hostel and campsite at Powers the Pot, but the Munster

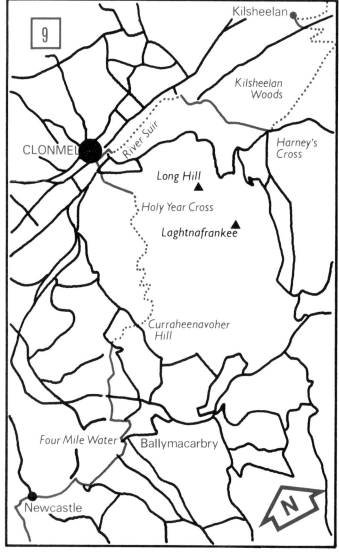

Way turns right instead and wanders down the minor road.

The road leads down across the slopes near Raven's Rock and plunges back into the forest before reaching the R680 road. Turn left to follow this road, then continue straight onwards along a narrow road to cross Sir Thomas Bridge. Turn left after crossing this narrow span to follow another stretch of path alongside the River Suir. This is a popular promenade for the inhabitants of Clonmel, so the way is largely paved and on reaching town the whole riverside has been extensively refurbished. A Tourist Information Office is one of the first buildings you'll have your attention drawn towards on entering the town. Clonmel is a major centre occurring at roughly the halfway point on the Coast to Coast Walk, and it offers a full range of shops, pubs, accommodation, bus and train services.

The River Suir

This river is the third of the "Three Sisters" along with its neighbours the Nore and Barrow. The Munster Way follows two parts of its old towpath on the journey from Carrick on Suir to Clonmel, and it is also seen briefly at Newcastle further along the walk. It rises by the curious Devilsbit Mountain and charts an even more curious course between ranges of hills before heading more directly towards Waterford Harbour and a confluence with the Nore and the Barrow.

Slievenamon

The solitary hump of Slievenamon resembles a huge, heathery breast crowned with a nipple of a cairn. Its name is derived from the Mountain of the Women. According to legend, women raced up the hill in a contest to see who would marry the hoary old warrior Fionn MacCumhail. The winner was Grainne, who had secretly been advised on tactics by Fionn himself. However, Grainne was soon running again, this time in a dramatic elopement with Diarmuid O'Dyna. Dozens of rocky slabs lying on remote mountainsides all around Ireland are styled as "Diarmuid and Grainne's Bed" and they no doubt had to keep on the move to avoid the ultimate wrath of Fionn. An annual hill race has recently been instituted on Slievenamon using the broad track ascending towards the summit from the village of Kilcash.

The Holy Year Cross is high on a hillside above Clonmel

Clonmel

This is the administrative town for the South Riding of Co Tipperary and is basically an Anglo-Norman town. It was walled after 1315 in response to the turmoil wreaked in Ireland by Edward Bruce. The walls you see near Old St Mary's Church, however, date from the 15th century, while the West Gate was built around 1830 on the site of an earlier gate. Cromwell besieged the town in 1650 and a garrison force has been present in the town since that time. Kickham Barracks dates from 1780 and passed from British control in 1922. It was rebuilt in the 1940s. The County Museum can offer more details about the development of the town. Charles Bianconi was operating a transport service out of Clonmel from 1815, while today there is a railway station offering links with places such as Dublin, Waterford, Cork and Limerick. Bus Eireann has plenty of daily and occasional services to many places and full details can be found by referring to table numbers 56, 66, 67, 68, 69, 84, 105, 113, 146 and 213. These transport services are especially useful if you decide to break the Coast to Coast Walk into two roughly equal stretches at this point.

DAY 12:
Clonmel to Clogheen
(*Sketch maps 9-10*)

Distance:	20 miles (32km).
Maps:	1:25,000 Comeragh Mountains Map (not an OS map).
	OS 1:50,000 Sheets 75 and 74.
	OS 1:126,720 Sheet 22.

Cross the River Suir via the Old Bridge to leave Clonmel. The road actually crosses two bridges as there is a sizeable island in the river. Once across the river you'll be facing a grotto and a nearby pub. There are three roads branching apart and you should take the middle one - which is to the right of the pub. As you walk along this road you pass a row of houses before taking another road off to the left. This is Roaring Spring Road and it climbs steeply uphill. You may spot a boundary stone affixed to a building and at that point you are passing from Co Tipperary into Co Waterford. Continue steeply uphill to pass a few farms, then look for a turning on the right. A stony track leads through a mass of rhododendrons on a hillside, then a path on the left squeezes between the bushes and climbs above them onto an open slope. The path leads straight up to the Holy Year Cross - a structure you may have identified already while walking alongside the River Suir near Clonmel.

As you pass the cross, swing to the right and climb over a heathery hump at 330m. As you descend from the hill, cross two fences and walk through some prickly gorse scrub to reach the corner of Cannon Hill Wood. At this point, turn left and follow an old track downhill. This passes a farm and continues downhill to reach Glenary River. You need to ford the river - which in very wet weather means wet feet. Alternatively, if the water is too high, you could retrace your steps and keep turning right to find an alternative crossing. Assuming you cross the ford, go straight through an iron gate and follow a grassy track uphill. When you reach a forest track, turn right to follow it across a deeply-cut stream, then turn left as the Munster Way climbs up another forest track.

The track climbs uphill and you should avoid a turning to the right, but keep going uphill. There is a broad zig-zag as the track makes height, then you should turn right at a junction around 325m. The track passes through a clear-felled area and contours around the hillside at the head of a broad valley. Don't take the track off to the right, but keep straight onwards to descend at a more gradual gradient to cross a minor road. Once across this road, the track leads around the northern side of Curraheenavoher Hill, and you should turn right at a junction with another forest track. This leads to another minor road, where you turn left, but almost immediately head off to the right along another minor road. This road leads down from the forest into the Nire Valley, passing through farmlands and later going through a staggered crossroads to continue downhill at a more gentle gradient. Turn left at another road junction to reach a tiny village at Four Mile Water, where there is a small shop. Turn right at this point, then left along another road to cross Four Mile Water Bridge, which spans the River Nire.

Turn right after crossing the Nire, passing a small pub and keeping right at the next junction, where you cross back from Co Waterford into Co Tipperary. The road rises, then a right turn leads down past Bannard House. Turn left along the next road, which leads into the village of Newcastle. Here, you could break for food and drink, or take advantage of accommodation in the surrounding area. To continue along the Munster Way, however, you leave Newcastle by following the road past the ruins of an old chapel, then turn left along a narrow road signposted for Mount Melleray Monastery. This road runs towards the slopes of the Knockmealdown Mountains, crossing Glenboy River and climbing parallel to the watercourse for a while. Later, there is a steeper climb to the right, away from the river, up the slopes of Knockroe. You need to look out for a turning off to the right, just before a row of black and yellow bollards are reached by the roadside at a farm access road.

A grassy trackway flanked with gorse bushes leads uphill and away from the road, and eventually bends left to climb past an old shooting lodge. The track continues to the corner of a forest, then turns right and wanders downhill alongside the forest fence. You cross the fence at a stile after sampling good views around the Comeragh and Galty Mountains. Turn left as soon as you land on a forest track and follow this downhill. It passes what appears to be a round tower, but is actually a monument to Liam Lynch - a Republican volunteer who was shot nearby. Continue down the forest track, then turn right and zig-zag down towards the Glengalla River. You cross the line of Rian Bo Phadraig - the Track of St Patrick's Cow - as you ford the river. A track rises towards a concrete water tank on the hillside, but you must head off to the right along a lesser track. Stay low in the forest and watch carefully for waymarks, as some are now hidden behind the branches of trees which have sprouted across the places where they have been erected. Also watch carefully for the course of the Munster Way after crossing a small river flowing down from Roche's Hill. The route enters a rather messy clear-felled area as it crosses the river and you should follow the rutted track back towards the trees and turn right along a better track. Later, there is a crossroads of forest tracks, where you should head straight onwards across the forested lower slopes of the mountains. Cross the river in Glenmoylan and turn left to walk uphill roughly parallel to it. Bear right later to reach a hairpin bend on the R668 road below the Vee Gap. Follow the road downhill to a junction with a minor road at the entrance to Glenlough, just next to a stone bridge on a pronounced bend in the road. The Munster Way ends at this road junction, where a final Munster Way mapboard can be viewed. Above is the Vee Gap, but at this point you will probably wish to follow the R668 road down towards the village of Clogheen for a night's accommodation. The village also has a few shops and pubs. In the morning, you would need to return to this road junction to continue along the next stage of the Coast to Coast Walk, which uses the Avondhu Way to proceed along the Knockmealdown Mountains and beyond Fermoy.

Comeragh Mountains Map

Although the Ordnance Survey have published a new 1:50,000 map covering the Comeragh Mountains, there is also a 1:25,000 map available which has been published privately. This double-sided map offers exceptional detail, from the intricate mosaic of field boundaries to the broad, bleak and boggy crest of the Comeragh Mountains. The style of the map is similar to that favoured by orienteers, so it comes as no surprise to find that Pat Healy - a noted

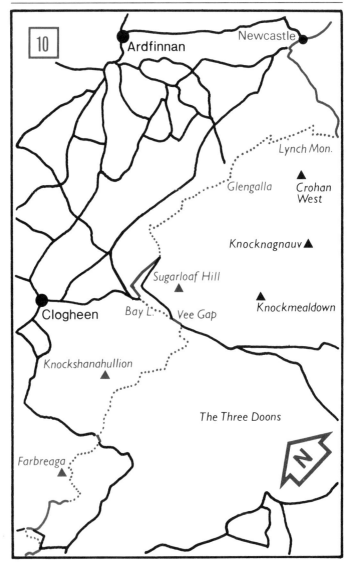

orienteer - actually drafted the map. Funding for the production of the map was provided by Eileen Ryan of Clonanav Farm Guesthouse in the Nire Valley near Ballymacarbry, with some assistance from Bord Failte. The course of the Munster Way is shown from Kilsheelan to Four Mile Water and the map reveals all the fiddly route details over the hills and through the forest on that stretch. The map has also been used on successive Lowe Alpine Two Day Mountain Challenges.

Holy Year Cross
This was constructed in 1950 and the surrounding Stations of the Cross were added in 1953. The structure is looking rather weather-beaten, but is maintained by people living on the southern bank of the River Suir at Clonmel. Thousands of worshippers climb up the moorland slope to hear Mass on the August Bank Holiday Monday each year.

Rian Bo Phadraig
The track of St Patrick's Cow is an ancient road across a gap in the heathery Knockmealdown Mountains. You cross its course as you reach the ford across the Glengalla River on the Munster Way. The ancient track has been included in a new waymarked route called St Declan's Way, which starts on the south coast at Ardmore and runs northwards across the Knockmealdown Mountains to reach the celebrated Rock of Cashel.

Clogheen
This little village is off-route, but it offers the only accommodation, shops and pubs for some distance on either the Munster Way or the Avondhu Way. Bus Eireann table numbers 68, 105 & 146 serve the village - the first offering a Tuesday only link with Clonmel, and the other two offering daily services to places such as Clonmel, Cork and Kilkenny. Unfortunately, no bus services cross the Vee Gap, though this is a popular run for holiday coaches. It is useful if you can arrange for some sort of transport to and from the route if you are staying overnight at Clogheen. There may in fact be a waymarked spur between the Vee Gap and Clogheen soon developed for walkers.

THE AVONDHU WAY

DAY 13:
Clogheen to Fermoy
(Sketch maps 10-11)

Distance: 25 miles (40km).

Maps: OS 1:50,000 Sheets 74 and 81 (not yet published).
OS 1:126,720 Sheet 22.

The Avondhu Way runs from the Vee Gap to Ballyhooly. This stage from the Vee Gap to Fermoy may seem long, but in fact the ground conditions are very good throughout and you should be able to maintain a good, steady pace. It helps, at the start of the day, if you can be given a lift up the R668 road from Clogheen to the start of the walk in the morning. A path climbs uphill to the right of the Munster Way mapboard. The path runs between gorse bushes and rhododendrons to reach Bay Lough, which is a lovely pool of water beneath a roughly vegetated slope. A good track continues uphill at a gentler gradient and reaches the highest part of the R668 road as it crosses the Vee Gap through the Knockmealdown Mountains at nearly 350m. A grotto stands a little way up the slopes from a car park, while across the road a steep and stony path can be seen climbing straight up the slopes of the Sugarloaf.

The Avondhu Way follows the road only a short way across the Vee Gap, then heads off to the right and climbs across a slope towards a forest. A stony pull leads uphill to the top corner of the forest, where you turn left. Walk alongside the edge of the forest, then drop down the slope to land on a track which you will find rising from the forest. Turn right to follow this track uphill and away from the forest. The track runs up a rugged hillside and passes through a gate in a fence near a broad moorland gap. Continue straight onwards across the heathery slopes of Knockaunabulloga at around 510m, then follow the track down to a junction. Turn right at this point, then right again along the edge of a young forest. Turn left around a far corner of the forest and continue walking alongside the fence. At the next corner of the forest, you should head uphill, following a line of waymark posts up the heathery slopes of Knockshanahullion. The Avondhu Way climbs to 600m and links with a bog road at a series of turf cuttings high on the hillside.

Follow the stony bog road downhill and join a narrow road which rises to cross a broad gap on the crest of the hills. Turn left and walk a short way along this road, then turn right to follow a track away from the road. This track crosses ground which has been recently planted with trees which are still very small. The track runs across moorland slopes and climbs towards Farbreaga, which can be distinguished by the cairn on its summit. The Avondhu Way passes close to the twin summits which rise to around 520m, before running downhill. As the track descends, look out for a sudden left turn where the route leaves the obvious track and follows a line of waymark posts down a broad, heathery spur. Another old track is joined and this continues downhill, swinging right later to lead across a slope between the open moorland and enclosed pastures. The route leaves the open slope and joins a minor road at a high corner.

Turn right and keep high on this road for some time, then turn off to the left to go down a forest track. This track simply zig-zags down to a lower minor road, where you turn right. Again, keep high on this road across the slopes of Carran Hill. The farm of Barnahoun on this road offers B&B for passing wayfarers, which proves useful on this long stretch as there is no other accommodation close to the route in the Araglin Valley. In fact, the only other facility comes in the shape of a pub far below in the scattered village of Araglin.

After passing the farm, the road turns right, then left, and passes a clear-felled forest. Turn left at the next road junction and follow a minor road downhill, then turn right along a high-banked trackway. As you near the end of this track, turn right up a much narrower path between the fields, then head left across the upper slopes of the hill. A winding track will lead you down past clumps of gorse, from Co Tipperary into Co Cork, then left along a farm track to reach another minor road. Turn right up this road, then left along another road. As this road later turns left to go downhill, you should

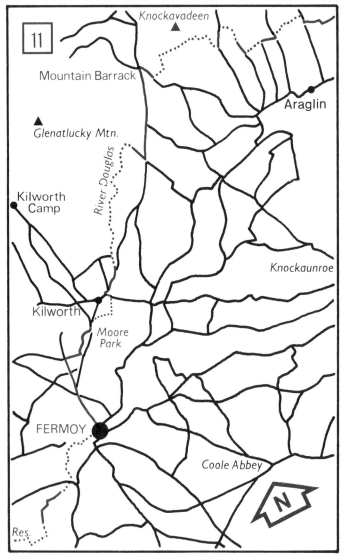

immediately go through a gate on the right and continue along an old, stony track. This leads through to a junction where you turn right and walk along a broad track next to a forest, with a view left across a deep-cut valley at Lyre.

Look for a stile on the left, where markers show the way down through the fields, crossing old walls and passing clumps of gorse. A step-stile leads down to a small stream, which you need to ford. Climb up the field beyond to reach another narrow minor road and turn left to follow it. There are fine views back into the deep-cut valley, then you turn off to the right along a winding track. Keep right at the next major junction of tracks and as you follow the track along the crest passing several fields, views of the Knockmealdown Mountains recede and there is a sudden view of the Galty Mountains. Don't take the first track off to the left, but keep left later until you reach a minor road, then turn right to follow this to a crossroads at Mountain Barrack. The Mountain Barrack Inn is immediately to hand if refreshments are needed, but to continue the walk you turn left along a fairly straight road. Walk along this road, which passes a modern house with fine gates, then there is a gradual descent towards a Keane's Cross Roads.

Turn right to follow a narrow minor road towards a forest, passing a large red notice warning of a firing range ahead. Don't worry, as you turn left only a short way beyond the sign and follow a forest track downhill. The track runs through a valley which has quite an open prospect and a variety of trees. The track stays fairly close to the River Douglas, crossing bridges where necessary, to reach a car park and picnic area where an information board gives brief details of other walks through the forest. As you exit from the car park onto a minor road, turn right and follow the road uphill. This eventually leads to the little village of Kilworth. Food and drink can be obtained at this point, but there is no accommodation. Turn left on reaching Kilworth, then turn right to follow the road into the grounds of Moore Park. Towards the end of this road, turn right to leave Moore Park, heading for a minor road which joins the main N8 road near a bridge.

Turn left to follow the busy N8 road only across the River Funshion, then turn right to follow the old road which has now been completely isolated by the more recent by-pass. The road rises back to the N8, near a handy B&B. Minor roads keeping well to the right of the busy N8 are used, and an old chapel is passed. A final descent leads into the town, which spreads across both sides of the River Blackwater and offers plenty of accommodation, shops and pubs for passing walkers.

Mountain Barrack

Although the pub at the crossroads bears the name of Mountain Barrack Inn, the actual barracks referred to are across the road and are no longer in use. They were established on this remote stretch of road, which was once the main Cork to Dublin highway, but the present main road is now some distance away and passes through Mitchelstown. You may notice an additional waymark at the crossroads, because although the Avondhu Way turns left at that point, there is a link which can be made with the distant Ballyhoura Way by turning right. The Ballyhoura Way is in turn expected to extend its distance and is an integral part of the O'Sullivan Beare Way, which will stretch from Glengarriff in Co Cork to Co Leitrim when completed. It is intended to recreate the bitter march endured by the O'Sullivan Beare clan, who cov-ered the distance during 1601

and 1602, losing about a thou-sand people to hunger, cold and ambushes, until only a handful reached the comparative safety of Co Leitrim.

Kilworth

Kilworth is a pleasant little village with shops and pubs, but

The Mountain Barrack Inn offers wayside refreshment to walkers

no accommodation. Bus Eireann table number 146 offers a sparse service to places such as Mitchelstown, Fermoy and Cork, but this is not available on Sundays. Nearby, but well out of sight, is Kilworth Camp. Soldiers from the camp are trained on a series of ranges, which are surrounded by warning notices - some of which are passed on the Avondhu Way near Douglas Water.

Fermoy
There is a grand entrance to Fermoy as walkers come down a steep hill, cross a fine bridge over the River Blackwater, then have the three sides of Pearse Square rising above and around them. The layout of the town practically demands that you pause and admire the buildings before moving onwards. There is accommodation, a range of shops and pubs, and good transport links. Bus Eireann table numbers, 77, 85, 105, 106 and 146 offer services to places such as Cork, Dublin, Waterford, Kilkenny, Mallow and Athlone throughout the week.

DAY 14:
Fermoy to Mallow
(Sketch maps 11-12)

Distance:	20 miles (32km).
Maps:	OS 1:50,000 Sheets 80 and 81 (not yet published).
	OS 1:126,720 Sheets 21 and 22.

The Avondhu Way extends beyond Fermoy to the village of Ballyhooly, but then there is a gap in the waymarked chain of trails which are linked on this Coast to Coast Walk across Ireland. The next waymarked trail is the Duhallow Way, which starts near the village of Bweeng. Until a route has been negotiated and waymarked between Ballyhooly and Bweeng, it might be best to follow a series of minor roads which can be linked via the town of Mallow. The unmarked gap in the Coast to Coast Walk is therefore filled with

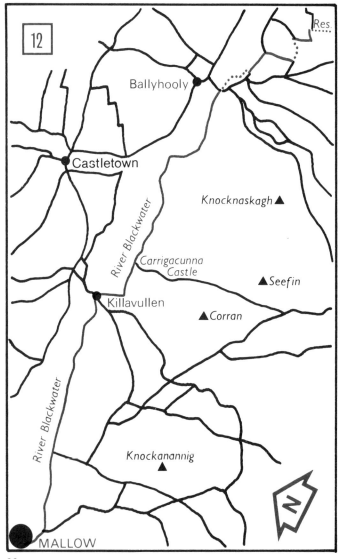

about 20 miles (32km) of road walking, mainly along the foot of the Nagles Mountains and generally parallel with the course of the River Blackwater.

As you cross the River Blackwater in Fermoy, turn left along the scenic Baranane Walk - a popular riverside promenade which is often busy with strollers and fishermen. This easy walk passes an old well, but then a stile suddenly leads walkers into a rather muddy area. The path continues alongside the River Blackwater through a couple of fields, then the Avondhu Way is routed through a structure known locally as "The Cage". This is where a right-of-way has been fenced in and screened from the view of a house. There is even a concrete tunnel to pass through, and enough quick-growing shrubs have been planted to ensure that it will one day become a rather dark and gloomy walk. Anyway, this part of the walk is fairly short and the path climbs up to a minor road. Turn right along this road and cross a nearby bridge, then turn left to enter a forest. Branch up to the right at some forestry huts and follow a narrower track up to another minor road. Turn left to follow the road uphill, noting that it makes a sudden sharp left and right turn. Further up this road, turn left and follow an access road up past a farm. Look out for a forest track on the right after passing the farm. The track leads straight into the forest, then you should turn left at the next junction of tracks. After turning left, follow the track until you can turn right along another track. You pass through a farmyard and follow the farm access road down to meet a minor road.

Turn left to walk down the minor road a short way. Turn right at the next junction and follow a narrow road more steeply downhill into a wooded valley. As soon as you cross a bridge over a river, turn left onto a forest track. Simply follow the track up through the valley, which has been partially clear-felled, and avoid a track which climbs up to the right. The route eventually leads out onto a minor road above the valley. Turn right to follow the road downhill, then turn left along a lower road. This leads to Gurteen Wood, which you can enter at a corner on the right side of the road. Walk along inside the wood, roughly parallel to the road, until you meet the forest track which enters the wood from the roadside. Turn right and follow the forest track gently downhill. Turn left later and follow the track onwards until you have to ford a stream at the edge of the wood. Turn right to follow the road to Bloomfield Crossroads, where the Castle Tavern offers accommodation near Ballyhooly.

The Avondhu Way ends at this point although there will one day be a waymarked continuation. Food, drink and lodgings are available at the pub, or you could cross the fine bridge over the River Blackwater and climb up to Ballyhooly village. You might also note the castle which is perched on a steep slope overlooking the river.

To make progress towards Mallow - and beyond to the start of the Duhallow Way - you can follow the minor road from the pub which is signposted for Killavullen. This road stays fairly close to the River Blackwater and passes through a forest before passing a number of farms and houses. There are pleasant views of the forested slopes of the Nagles Mountains, rising to open moorlands above the trees. Later, on the right, you may catch a glimpse of Carrigacunna Castle. The road turns sharply right after the castle and descends to the village of Killavullen. A few shops and pubs can be found in this quiet little place, but there is no accommodation. Turn left in Killavullen and follow the minor road signposted for Mallow. Be sure to stay on the road which runs to the right side of a church as you leave the village. The Nagles Mountains now feature only in retrospect, and you'll later find yourself following the tall wall bounding Rockforest House. The road descends and passes a pub and features a short stretch of the River Blackwater. The busy N20 road is finally joined and this leads across a bridge into the main part of Mallow. A full range of accommodation, shops and pubs are available for walkers.

Mallow

Mallow is a splendid shopping centre and it has grown up around a now-defunct spa. The town was, however, founded much earlier and it features a castle which was built in the 16th century. The full range of shops makes this an ideal point for stocking up on supplies as there are few facilities along the Duhallow Way. If a break of journey is required, then Bus Eireann table numbers 77, 111, 148, 152 and 153 offer a range of services to points such as Cork, Waterford, Limerick, and even far northwards to Galway, Westport and Ballina. Table number 152 offers a Saturday only link with the village of Killavullen. There is also a railway station in town.

THE DUHALLOW WAY

Distance: 18 miles (29km).

Maps: OS 1:50,000 Sheet 80 (not yet published).
                OS 1:126,720 Sheet 21.

The Duhallow Way starts on the slopes of Bweeng Mountain near the village of Bweeng and runs as far as the Clydagh Valley in Co Kerry. The first task on the Coast to Coast Walk is to get from Mallow to Bweeng Mountain, as there is no waymarked trail. However, a series of fairly quiet roads can be followed to effect a link. If you are leaving the centre of Mallow, then you need to cross over the River Blackwater on the main N20 road. Turn right along a road which keeps roughly parallel to the river as it leaves town. The road goes under a tall railway viaduct and crosses the Clyda River. Continue straight onwards to pass a sugar factory, then turn left and walk over a railway crossing. The road rises through the crossroads village of Drommahane, where you go straight through before turning off to the right along the R619 road. There is a shop in the village if anything is required.

The road runs away from Drommahane and continues through a crossroads before making a pronounced bend around the River Lyre. Ballysimon Cross Roads is reached next, where you should turn right, but not sharply right, along a minor road. This road turns left and right before climbing slightly to a junction. Turn left to continue, crossing the infant River Lyre again, then keeping straight onwards to climb towards the forested flanks of Bweeng Mountain. When you reach a road junction, turn right, then after passing a farm, bear left at a fork in the road. A forest track later heads off to the left and this is the start of the Duhallow Way. The Coast to Coast Walk is once again able to follow a waymarked trail. If extra confirmation of the forest track is required, then it is the one which is flanked by a line of telegraph poles, as well as way-marked posts.

Follow the for-est track uphill and off to the right, keeping the telegraph poles alongside as you proceed. As the track climbs up through the forest, there are occasional views out to the surrounding countryside. The telegraph poles actually run to the prominent masts which stand on the 417m summit of Bweeng Mountain, but the Duhallow Way doesn't actually climb all the way to the top. Instead, the route turns off to the left and goes down another forest track. After descending this track, turn left along another track and follow this out into a minor road known as French's Road. Turn left again along French's Road, then turn right along another forest track further along the road. This track climbs a little way, then swings to the right across a clear-felled crest. The track runs high for a while, then descends to a minor road in a quiet little valley. Turn left to walk up the narrow minor road and pass a couple of ruined farmsteads. Note a tabular block of rock across the road from a solitary cottage, then follow the road across a river.

A track on the right climbs into another forest, then a left turn leads along a forest ride which has some rather rough and boggy patches along its length. Forge onwards, crossing a boggy watercourse and cutting straight across other forest rides. When you reach the edge of the forest you turn right to walk along a firm bog Road. The broad bogland above the village of Nad features a number of criss-cross tracks and turf cuttings. As you walk along the bog road, look out for a turning on the left and follow this uphill. Next, you need to turn right, then left along another bog road. You should find yourself being led down from the bog to reach the R579 road. Turn right to follow this road gradually downhill.

This is far enough for one day, but there are no nearby lodgings at the moment. The nearest settlement is at Glenaknockane, then there is the tiny village of Nad, which has a pub, but it is even further to Banteer and a rather limited range of accommodation. It might be a good idea to phone ahead from Mallow and check the range of accommodation, book an appropriate place to stay, and enquire whether you can be collected from a point on the R579 road above

A turf cutting on the broad boglands high above the village of Nad

Glenaknockane and taken down to your lodgings. If you have to walk all the way down to Banteer, you can expect to finish late and be somewhat footsore into the bargain. There are plans to establish some sort of accommodation for walkers near Nad, and with a bit of luck a farmhouse B&B might be available nearer to Glenaknockane.

Duhallow

Duhallow is the name of an ancient barony in West Cork and the name has recently been applied to the Duhallow Way. This trail has been developed by IRD Duhallow - with IRD standing for Integrated Resource Development - and with a highly successful EU LEADER Programme in place the establishment of the route has been quick and efficient. A number of countryside projects are being developed in the area, such as the Millstreet Country Park, the provision of rural accommodation and the collection of folklore and history. As each development proceeds apace, there is a need for training, funding and job creation and it is fair to say that IRD Duhallow has one of the best organised and most successful programmes in Ireland.

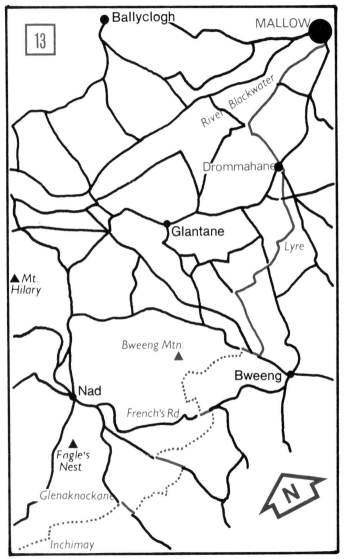

DAY 16:
Glenaknockane to Millstreet
(Sketch maps 13-14)

Distance: 17 miles (27km).

Maps: OS 1:50,000 Sheet 80 (not yet published) and 79.
OS 1:126,720 Sheet 21.

As you come down towards Glenaknockane along the R579 road, a track leads off to the left alongside a small forest. The track passes through a forest for a short while, then continues as a bog road across a broad slope of heathery ground. Later, the track descends to cross a river, then rises to pass into another forest. There is a left turn down another track inside the forest, then a walk along a rather boggy forest ride. Cross a stream on this ride and walk up to cross the fence at the edge of the forest above Inchimay. Turn right to walk across the rough moorland slope roughly parallel to the forest fence. There is a boggy, rutted track covered in heather, which makes walking quite difficult, then there is a stream to cross which is rather awkward as it runs through a steep-sided cutting. Once across the stream, a bog road can be followed and this offers a much firmer footing and allows for a quicker pace. The bog road crosses the Ownagluggin River and runs uphill a short way. Turn left along another narrow road and follow this back across the Ownagluggin River. The road continues uphill past a series of turf cuttings, then you turn right along another stretch of road. Take the next track rising off to the left, and follow this past a number of near-exhausted turf cuttings to reach a forest at a gate.

Enter the forest and follow the track uphill. Turn sharply right along another track and contour around the forested hillside. Look out for a path on the right which leaves the track and runs to the edge of the forest. Waymarks show how the Duhallow Way crosses a broad and boggy slope towards the broad rise of Seefin, where a bog road is joined. Don't be drawn off to the right towards the summit of Seefin, but keep to the bog road as it descends gradually across the slopes of the hill. It lands on a minor road at a small car park on a high gap between the hills around 430m. Ahead is the huge hump of Musheramore, which the Duhallow Way cuts across, first by climbing up the rugged slopes of Mushera. Look carefully ahead for waymark posts, which will lead you around the hill and take you as high as 480m at the head of a little valley cut into the hillside. After crossing a fence, the route stays high above a forest, but then starts to descend along a rough track and eventually runs into the forest. On the way, there is a view of John's Well, where the Stations of the Cross have been arranged in a clearing in the forest. The Duhallow Way runs down to a junction of forest tracks, where you should turn left after crossing a stile. A track leads away from the edge of the forest and crosses a field. The route crosses one last rough patch of ground before landing on a minor road near a road junction on a gap at around 380m.

Take the minor road which runs towards Knocknakilla Stone Circle. This road cuts across the northern slopes of Musherabeg and looks down on the new Millstreet Country Park - a development which fills a broad valley below the hill. Knocknakilla Stone Circle is signposted on the left side of the road and a short path leads to the great tilted upright stone and a number of squat specimens nearby. Continue down the road, which passes through a forest, then turn left at the next road junction. You may notice the top of another standing stone off to the left side of the road. Turn right along the next road and follow it gently downhill. Another right turn seems to lead only along a farm access road, but before you reach the farm you continue along a grassy track from a gateway and off to the left past an uninhabited building at Carrigacooleen.

The track leads onto a minor road, where a right turn commences the long descent by road towards Millstreet. Avoid all turnings to the left and right and head through Cloghboola More and across the Minister's Bridge. When you reach a roadside grotto at a junction of roads, the Duhallow Way actually turns sharply left along the R582 road. However, you will probably want to head into Millstreet, so you follow the main road straight onwards to reach the town, which can offer the weary wayfarer accommodation, food and drink.

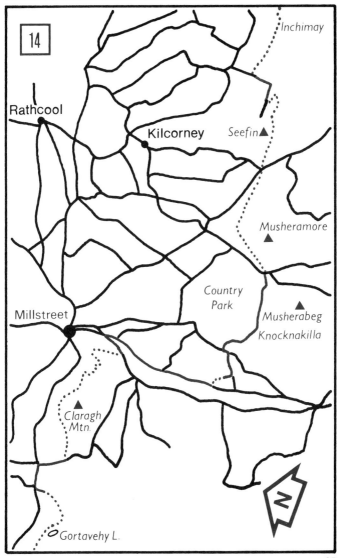

Millstreet

For a town of small stature, Millstreet achieved European fame as the venue for the 1993 Eurovision Song contest - at which Ireland won...yet again! It had been unkindly described as being "on the bog road to Killarney". It crouches at the foot of Claragh Mountain and the development of both the Duhallow Way and the nearby Millstreet Country Park should serve to attract more walkers into the area. There is a railway station outside of town which offers services to Killarney, Tralee, Cork and Dublin. Bus Eireann table numbers 101, 109, 110 and 176 offer services to places such as Cork, Killarney and Tralee, but table number 110 offers a summer service as far north as Galway, while table number 101 offers a service from coast to coast across Ireland from Tralee to Rosslare Harbour. You might like to bear this in mind as the Coast to Coast Walk draws to a close.

DAY 17:
Millstreet to Loo Bridge
(Sketch maps 14-15)

Distance:	22 miles (36km).
Maps:	OS 1:50,000 Sheet 79.
	OS 1:126,720 Sheet 21.

The Duhallow Way continues from Millstreet to the Clydagh Valley, where it ends suddenly with no accommodation or other nearby facilities. Walkers will naturally continue along the length of the Clydagh Valley to reach the main road at Clonkeen, and by continuing along the road towards Killarney they will find a couple of roadside B&Bs. A youth hostel can be found at Loo Bridge on the Kenmare road. Although there is an unmarked gap between the Duhallow Way and the Kerry Way, this is easily filled by using roads for a while.

Follow the R582 road southwards out of Millstreet, as if for

Following the bog road from Knockshanahullion towards Farbreaga (Day 13)

Traditional Irish pub frontage in the village of Ballyhooly (Day 14)

Following the Duhallow Way across Claragh Mountain above Millstreet (Day 17)

The jagged crest of MacGillycuddy's Reeks rises above the Black Valley (Day 18)

Macroom, to join the Duhallow Way at the roadside grotto. Look out for a turning on the right further along the road, where the route is taken across a number of fields. The route passes in front of a large ruined house at Mountleader, then a left turn and a right turn lead up across more fields. When a track is joined, turn left to follow it, then turn right to continue up a track which passes a number of trees on a steep slope. At the top of this slope, look for a stile just off to the left and cross it. You appear to be heading straight towards Claragh Mountain, but the Duhallow Way heads off to the right for a while, then swings round to the left to follow a track lower down the hillside. This track is delightfully grassy and it cuts across the mid-slope of Claragh Mountain before ascending to follow the upper edge of a small forest. Look for a marker on the left which indicates that you should leave the track and cut across the broad, heathery slopes of the hill. There are some clumps of gorse along the way, and ahead there is a fine view of Caherbarnagh's rugged face, towards which the Duhallow Way is heading. The path drifts gradually downhill from the heathery slopes and leads around a slope to cross a small valley. A minor road is joined just beyond the valley, where you turn right to walk downhill.

At Croohig's Cross Roads, turn left to walk across Ahaphooca Bridge. Another left turn leads up a farm access road which becomes a track climbing up through fields towards the heathery heights again. Beware of fences along this stretch of the walk, as they may be electrified. Swing to the right as you climb up the heathery slopes above the fields, maybe reaching as high as 370m before descending along a spur towards Gortavehy Lough. A track leads down towards the lough, which nestles in a hollow below the frowning face of Stoukeen - a rugged shoulder of Caherbarnagh. Cross the outflow from the lough, then cross a fence and contour around the rugged hillside at around 300m. Markers are sparse, but the fence which crosses this rugged slope will lead you onwards to cross a small stream which runs through a fairly deep cut. Climb uphill from the stream to reach a crest overlooking Lough Murtagh, which is couched in a small hollow in the hills.

As you follow fences onwards around the slopes of Glanaprehane - another shoulder of Caherbarnagh - you may notice the twin peaks of The Paps rising in the distance. The waymarked path climbs above the level of the fence and almost touches 400m before descending towards a valley. Cross a stile in the fence, then look carefully ahead for markers as the Duhallow Way crosses a rough and rocky slope. This is awash with small streams and some of the rocks being crossed could prove to be very slippery. Don't be tempted to short-cut into the valley either, as there is even rougher ground which is just out of sight below. When you reach the bottom of the slope, turn right and ford the small river in the valley. After admiring views around the rugged head of the valley, continue up a boggy, roughly vegetated slope. The Duhallow Way crosses from Co Cork into Co Kerry as it runs northwards along the edge of a forest. There is some prickly gorse scrub to pass through before there is a left turn around the corner of the forest. A track is crossed at the next corner, above a small farm at Awnaskirtawn, then a descent leads across ruined walls around a number of fields. The fields contain massive cairns which have been formed from the clearing of stones from the ground. A stream is crossed in the valley, then the route climbs up a broad and boggy slope. The Paps loom large over the landscape, but the route seems to swing off to the right to avoid them. After passing around a farmhouse, there is a very narrow road to cross before the route drops down into another valley. Watch carefully for waymarks across the valley, then climb up the other side.

You should take the time to explore The City at this point, which is revealed as a large, circular stone structure in the shadow of The Paps. It has always been a most important religious site and is worth a few moments of study. To continue along the Duhallow Way, however, you need to turn left as you climb up from the valley. The path passes a few trees above the edge of the valley, but is ultimately drawn downhill across a rugged slope to cross the Beheenagh River. The path climbs up to join a rough track, and by turning right you can follow this towards the elongated pool of Shrone Lake. This rough, bouldery, heathery glen is known as the Sloigeadal, and the track passes through it quite easily. Although the track is low in the glen at first, it climbs up a steep and rocky slope and eventually crosses a high gap between The Paps and Knocknabro. A gate is passed on top of the gap and the track passes a forest for a short while as it descends into the Clydagh Valley. The route lands on a

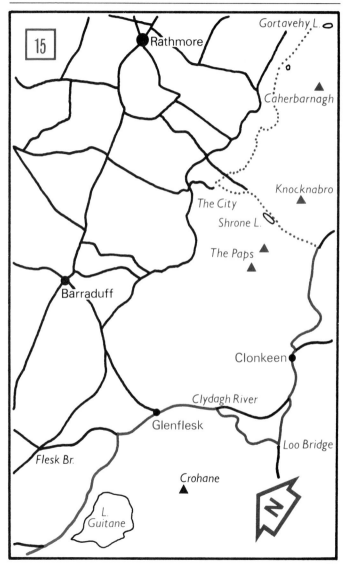

15

Rathmore

Gortavehy L.

Caherbarnagh

Knocknabro

The City

Shrone L.

The Paps

Barraduff

Clonkeen

Clydagh River

Glenflesk

Loo Bridge

Flesk Br.

Crohane

L. Guitane

N

minor road in the valley, where the Duhallow Way comes to an abrupt end with no facilities in sight.

The obvious way to continue without the benefits of a waymarked trail is to turn right and follow the narrow, twisting minor road through the Clydagh Valley. Although there are farms along the way, and some improved pasture, the overall aspect of the valley is quite rugged. The road crosses a bridge over a rocky gorge as it finally debauches from the valley and joins the main N22 road at Clonkeen. Turn right to start walking down this road, which runs down towards Killarney in due course. A church is passed, then more of the buildings which make up the straggly settlement of Clonkeen. It is best to keep to the right side of the road, facing the oncoming traffic, as there are a number of bends and the road can be quite busy. You won't need to follow the road too far as you can take the Kenmare road - the R569 - which is signposted off to the left. This leads past a small shop, then past a pub, then reaches the youth hostel at Loo Bridge. There is, therefore, just enough in the way of facilities to feed, water and house you for the night. If the youth hostel is closed, then turn left along a narrow minor road, but *not* the one which crosses Loo Bridge, and follow this towards Woodgrove Farm B&B for the night instead.

The City
Strange things have taken place at The City over the past number of centuries. This ancient religious site has been created at the foot of The Paps and those overshadowing twin peaks, which rise like enormous breasts, may have encouraged the development of an "Earth Mother" system of beliefs and rituals. It has been recorded that cattle were later penned into the large, circular stone fort in order to obtain a whole year's miraculous protection from disease. These days, "cures" are still taken from the stones, but the emphasis now is more penitential. This is a pattern which has been repeated at several sites across Ireland. It seems that the early missionaries couldn't stop people from visiting the ancient sites, so they simply "Christianised" them and encouraged a different system of beliefs on a pattern of ritual which may well have been quite similar to earlier pagan rituals.

St Patrick's Cabbage

This is a saxifrage which many gardeners will know as London Pride. Any bit of broken rock will allow it to flourish in most gardens. Its natural worldwide distribution, however, is really quite limited and unusual. It is a native of the south-west of Ireland and the high Pyrenees - which earns it the accolade of being a Hiberno-Lusitanian plant. It grows in profusion in the rocky mountains and valleys of the south-west of Ireland and becomes particularly noticeable during this day's walk. It starts by occupying space on rocky valley sides, crouches under boulders all through the Sloigeadal, then sprouts gloriously from roadside walls along the length of the Clydagh Valley. In fact, you should be able to find specimens all the way to the end of the Coast to Coast Walk through Co Kerry, and it is especially noticeable when it flowers in the early summer and seems to welcome walkers to this part of Ireland with its prominent, cheerful little blooms on long stalks.

The Spotted Slug

Another curious native of this part of the world is the Spotted Slug, or Kerry Slug. This is something to look for after days of heavy rain, when the ground is completely sodden and it may be noticed grazing lichen off the tops of rocks. On bright, clear days it prefers to keep deep down in the shade and so you wouldn't expect to see it at all. It has the status of being a protected species, but is hardly all that rare or threatened with extinction.

THE KERRY WAY

DAY 18:
Loo Bridge to The Black Valley
(Sketch maps 15-16)

Distance:	22 miles (36km).
Maps:	OS 1:25,000 Killarney National Park Map.
	OS 1:25,000 MacGillycuddy's Reeks Map.
	OS 1:50,000 Sheets 78 & 79.
	OS 1:63,360 Map of Killarney District.
	OS 1:126,720 Sheet 20.

The first part of this day's walk aims to use roads to reach the course of the Kerry Way at Muckross - just a short way from the actual starting point of the walk at Killarney. From that point, the Kerry Way will be followed as far as Cahersiveen, leaving only a short, unmarked stretch to bring the Coast to Coast Walk to a conclusion. Before you start today's walk, however, you should realise that accommodation in the remote Black Valley is limited to a single farmhouse B&B and a youth hostel - both of which can become fully booked in the summer months. It would be a good idea to book your bed in advance.

As you leave Loo Bridge Youth Hostel, turn right to follow a minor road which runs along the foot of an exceptionally steep and rugged slope. You may spot overhanging cliffs, enormous tumbled boulders, and a vegetation cover so tangled and barbed that it seems to deny all access. The minor road passes this awesome terrain with ease and passes Woodgrove Farm B&B before reaching the main N22 road. Turn left to follow this much improved road towards the tiny village of Glenflesk. There is a good-sized hard shoulder so that you can keep your distance from the traffic, and the road runs through a deep rock cutting before reaching Glenflesk. There is a small shop by the roadside, then the road continues towards

Killarney. You don't need to go into town, but turn off to the left instead and follow a minor road towards Muckross.

This minor road runs uphill and passes a number of houses and farms, then there are some fine views across Lough Guitane to the rugged stump of Bennaunmore and the taller peaks of Crohane and Stoompa. Mangerton Mountain also fills the sky with its bulk, while Purple Mountain and a glimpse of MacGillycuddy's Reeks feature more distantly. The road runs past Lough Guitane and crosses Finow Bridge. Don't turn left at the signpost for Peacock's Hostel, but turn left along the next road, which is signposted for Mangerton. This road runs along and climbs uphill a short way, crosses the Finoulagh River, then after another short rise it zig-zags down towards the main N71 road at Muckross. Cross over this road and use a nearby entrance to follow a tarmac pathway towards Muckross House. The course of the Kerry Way is joined quite close to the ruins of Muckross Abbey, which you could visit by making a short detour off to the right. Returning to the upper path, continue through the parkland and woodland, looking out for herds of Kerry cattle before making a left turn and walking straight towards Muckross House. The Coast to Coast Walk is again following a waymarked trail as it travels along the Kerry Way at Muckross.

Refreshments and interpretative displays are available at Muckross House, but the Kerry Way heads off to the right at a signpost for Torc Waterfall. Later, you turn left along another path and walk fairly close to the shore of Muckross Lake. This path, like many others around Muckross House, is used by jarveys and their horse-drawn jaunting cars. The path leads into a wooded area, then a tunnel allows you to pass beneath the main N71 road and continue straight onwards to view Torc Waterfall. The falls are best seen after heavy rain, particularly in winter when the overhanging trees are bare. The Kerry Way goes up a flight of stone steps, then zig-zags up a path and bears left to reach a car park. Turn right at that point and follow an obvious track across a bridge spanning the Owengarriff River. Climb up along the track, passing a variety of trees before reaching a barrier gate.

Beyond the gate is the open country of The Wilderness, where the Old Kenmare Road crosses a rugged moorland with ease. The broad track climbs gradually uphill, then descends to a terminus.

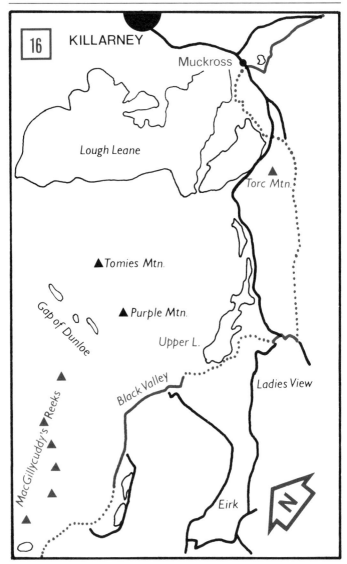

The Kerry Way proceeds along a narrower path and crosses a river using a footbridge. The path climbs up through the mossy, stony little Esknamucky Glen, emerging onto a boggy and overtrodden moorland slope. Forge across a broad gap at around 300m, then follow the path downhill. Another mossy woodland is negotiated and the rugged course of Galway's River is crossed by a footbridge. The woodland path finally descends to a narrow road in a valley clothed with rhododendrons. Turn right along this narrow road and walk down to the main N71 road by the old Derrycunnihy Church. Turn left along the main road at the church, but look out for a marker on the right which shows the way off the road and down through a wood. This stretch of the Kerry Way has abundant waymarks as the path twists and turns as it descends through the woods to reach the ruins of Queen's Cottage.

Turn left at the ruins to follow a broader, stonier track and follow this onwards through the mossy woodlands. The track later emerges from the trees and the gravelly surface allows an easy walk across the tussocky bogs near the Upper Lake. The Kerry Way passes through a gate and heads towards a wooded area, then passes through another gate and turns left. A track leads towards Lord Brandon's Cottage, where you can sometimes break for refreshments at a cafe. When you leave, cross a bridge over the Gearhameen River which has a fine gateway built into it. Turn left and walk along the road roughly parallel to the river. You eventually reach a road junction where you need to make a decision. Accommodation is limited to two addresses only. Either turn right to reach Hillcrest Farm B&B, or continue straight along the road, following the Kerry Way to the Black Valley Youth Hostel. There is a small shop next to the hostel, a nearby church and school, and a scattering of small farmhouses. Great stony slopes rise from the Black Valley to the majestic crest of MacGillycuddy's Reeks - the highest range of mountains in the whole of Ireland.

Muckross House

When Senator Arthur Vincent presented the Muckross Estate to the nation in 1932, he was actually laying the foundations for the growth of national parks throughout Ireland. As the estate was passed to the Commissioners for Public Works, it was stated that the

The rugged stump of Bennaunmore rises above Lough Guitane

area was to be managed "as a national park for the general purpose of the recreation and enjoyment of the public". Few people realise that Ireland actually had a national park many years before Britain, or that national parks in Ireland are wholly state-owned, rather than simply subject to planning restrictions. The Muckross Estate became known as the Bourn Vincent Memorial Park, but in the 1970s a number of other purchases of land increased the area, which was now under the control of the Office of Public Works, and the greater area was renamed as the Killarney National Park. Muckross House serves as the visitor centre for the park and has interpretative facilities and refreshments. Traditional crafts can also be studied nearby, while rare Kerry cattle graze in the surrounding grounds. In 1932, Senator Arthur Vincent said "I want especially to have the young people come to Muckross to trail those mountains and enjoy nature in all its aspects". Happily, this seems to be happening.

The Old Kenmare Road
This old road is used in its entirety by the Kerry Way, which wanders from Torc to Derrycunnihy on its outward journey, then

from Kenmare back to Torc on its return, after making a lengthy tour around the Iveragh peninsula. The use of the road was actually barred by a former landlord, so that families who lived along its length were unable to move any of their goods along it. They were then forced to leave their farmsteads, which are now visible only as crumbling ruins lost among the wild moorland vegetation. The area was managed as a red deer reserve, where pure Irish red deer were raised for hunting purposes. An alternative road was constructed between Kenmare and Killarney, and this is now the main N71 road. Although the Old Kenmare Road was in many places almost completely overwhelmed by the surrounding moorlands, it has in some measure been restored by having the Kerry Way routed along it. The stretch across the slopes of Torc Mountain has been completely resurfaced, and some limited resurfacing has been accomplished on other stretches. In some of the woodlands, the original stonework of the old road can be distinguished beneath the growths of moss.

The Upper Lake

The Upper Lake is approached quite closely by the Kerry Way for most of the year. However, the lakeshore is used for grazing by Whitefronted Geese each winter, which fly in from Greenland for the fodder thereabouts. A detour may be signposted in the winter months to avoid undue disturbance to the geese.

DAY 19:
The Black Valley to Glenbeigh
(Sketch maps 16-17)

Distance:	22 miles (36km).
Maps:	OS 1:25,000 MacGillycuddy's Reeks Map.
	OS 1:50,000 Sheet 78.
	OS 1:63,360 Map of Killarney District.
	OS 1:126,720 Sheet 20.

Continue walking along the road through the Black Valley, bearing

Mountains rise on almost every side around remote Glencar

left at a road junction where a cul-de-sac sign stands. The road runs past a number of small farms, then you need to keep right along another narrow road. This road passes more small farms, then it zig-zags uphill to continue as a forest walk. The Kerry Way is badly overtrodden in the forest, but there are plenty of stepping stones in the mud. When you leave the forest, continue across a bouldery hillside, aiming to the right of the steep-faced mountain of Broaghnabinnia which seems almost to block the head of the Black Valley. Eventually, you will pass a small house and join a narrow road. Turn right to follow this road uphill. It runs as a broad track towards the head of the Black Valley. At the end of the track are two buildings - one yellow and green and the other one red and white. Walk straight past them to continue across a slope. You need to bear left at a large boulder, then later cross a footbridge. The Kerry Way climbs up a vague path known as the Bridle Path, which zig-zags up a bouldery slope at the head of the valley. A high gap at nearly 300m is crossed and you should take care to keep well to the right of a prominent standing stone as you cross the gap.

The gap is situated between the bulky, bouldery Broaghnabinnia

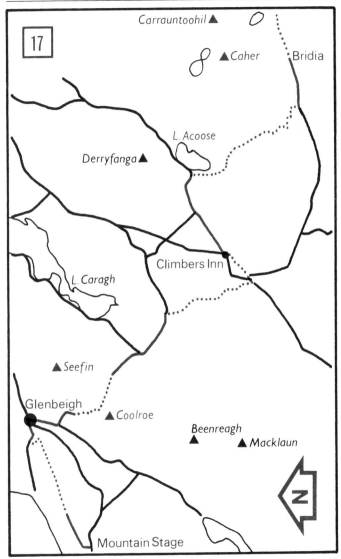

17

Carrauntoohil ▲

▲ *Caher*

Bridia

L. Acoose

Derryfanga ▲

Climbers Inn

L. Caragh

▲ *Seefin*

Glenbeigh

▲ *Coolroe*

Beenreagh
▲

▲ *Macklaun*

N

Mountain Stage

and the more distant peak of Caher - one of Ireland's highest mountains. A line of waymark posts cross the gap and show the way down into the Bridia Valley. A steep and rocky descent finally leads to a farm at the head of the valley and you walk away from it simply by following its access road. A couple of other farms are passed before the Kerry Way heads off to the right, away from the road. The ascent of the Lack Road is vague at first, so look carefully ahead for markers. A steep, grassy slope has to be climbed at first, then a more obvious old zig-zag track will be joined. Some parts of the track are rather boggy or indeterminate, but the marker posts will show you where to turn a corner as you zig-zag further uphill to gain height. Eventually, a rugged gap in the hills is reached at around 400m and a descent leads off down a very steep slope into a rugged glen. Again, there are zig-zags to ease the gradient. At some point you must stop and admire the impressively rugged slopes of Caher. Behind that mountain is Carrauntoohil, which is the highest mountain in Co Kerry, the Province of Munster, and indeed the whole of Ireland. It rises to a lofty peak of 1039m and could in fact be climbed from the top of the Lack Road.

The Lack Road makes a steeply zig-zagging descent, then runs out onto a more level valley floor to proceed as a fairly clear track alongside the Gearhanagour Stream. This track runs below an inhabited farmhouse, then passes an uninhabited one. Turn left and climb a short way above the track at this point, then bear to the right and contour around the rugged slope overlooking Lough Acoose. The track continues from the outflow to a minor road. Turn left along this road and follow it gradually downhill alongside a forest. Keep left at a road junction and continue along the road to reach the Climbers Inn at Glencar. There is a small shop attached to the pub, as well as accommodation. There are also a couple of B&Bs nearby if a break of journey is required on this long day.

If you're not stopping, then turn left at the Climbers Inn and follow an old track for a short way. This cuts out a bit of road walking and eventually you will reach a road which runs straight onwards to cross Bealalaw Bridge in a rugged, boggy area surrounded by ranges of mountains. Turn right immediately after crossing the bridge and follow the River Caragh downstream. After following the river through a rocky cut, the Kerry Way heads off to the left alongside a smaller stream and enters a forest. Continue walking along a forest track to reach a minor road. Turn right along this road, then turn off to the left to go up through an old gateway. A track zig-zags uphill into the trees, then a narrower path climbs up to a rocky viewpoint. You can look across Lough Caragh, or towards a trio of the highest mountains in Ireland - Beenkeragh, Carrauntoohil and Caher. A flight of steps leads down from the viewpoint, passing a sheer cliff and eventually leading down to another minor road. The Kerry Way turns left to follow the road across the Meelagh River and Owbeg River. The road climbs uphill, almost to a school near a roadside B&B. Turn left at the B&B and follow a narrower road further uphill. Views of the surrounding countryside begin to open up splendidly as the road approaches Gortdirragh.

There are two alternative ways of reaching Glenbeigh via the Kerry Way, and it is suggested that the shorter option is the one which is taken on this walk. Turn left to go through a gate, then follow a stony track which slants uphill across the heathery upper slopes of Seefin. This track climbs up to a gap between Seefin and Coolroe at nearly 350m. As you pass through the gap, you'll be able to look across Dingle Bay towards Brandon Mountain, which indicates that the Coast to Coast Walk across Ireland is rapidly reaching its end. The track descends across the top of Cummergorm Glen and zig-zags down the hillside. It joins a minor road, where a right turn leads towards Glenbeigh. The village offers accommodation, shops and pubs. Also, if you find yourself running short of time, you could end the Coast to Coast Walk by following the road down to the beach at Ross-Behy, and dip your feet into the sea off the White Strand. However, the Coast to Coast Walk can be brought to a more satisfying conclusion by continuing westwards to Cahersiveen and Valencia Island.

Carrauntoohil

Carrauntoohil is Ireland's highest mountain at 1039m. It often bears a cap of cloud and can be difficult to view if you are simply passing by it on the Kerry Way. The route actually passes quite close to the summit, but the approaches would need some considerable extra time as the slopes are steep and rugged. The view from the rocky viewpoint above Lough Caragh takes in the three highest mountains in Ireland - Beenkeragh at 1010m, Carrauntoohil at 1039m and Caher at 1001m. All three are arranged around Coomloughra, and the Coomloughra Horseshoe is reckoned to be one of the finest mountain walks in Ireland.

Glenbeigh

One of the growing attractions at Glenbeigh is the Bog Village. Here, a traditional village has been constructed using the 100 per cent recyclable materials of the Irish countryside. There is also a nature reserve along the beach road, on the sheltered marshes behind the protective barrier of Rosbehy Point and the White Strand. Bus Eireann table numbers 178 and 179 offer services to Killarney, Tralee and Cahersiveen, with no Sunday service and some seasonal variations.

DAY 20:
Glenbeigh to Cahersiveen
(Sketch maps 17-18)

Distance:	17 miles (27km).
Maps:	OS 1:50,000 Sheets 78 and 83.
	OS 1:126,720 Sheet 20.

The Kerry Way leaves Glenbeigh as if it is heading for the beach, but only follows the road as far as a picnic area at the foot of a forested slope. A path climbs uphill from the picnic area, then you turn left along a broader and more level path. Follow this onwards, watching for a turning on the right where a path climbs steeply to the upper edge of the forest. Cross the forest fence and continue steeply uphill following a path alongside another fence which rises through bracken and heather. The path is stony in places and eventually runs to a summit at 275m. On this ascent, there are good views back towards Glenbeigh, as well as to the surrounding mountains and across Dingle Bay towards more mountains. Descend alongside the fence from the summit of the hill, then cross the fence on a gap and head towards a track after contouring a short way around the southern slopes of the hill. This track leads down to a narrow minor road, which you follow straight onwards, as if heading for the shapely bulk of Drung Hill. A sudden left turn later takes this road across a bridge which spans a cutting where the main N70 Ring of Kerry road runs.

Turn right to follow another minor road parallel to the main road at Mountain Stage. There is a Civil War monument by the road. After following this road around a broad bend, you need to head off to the left, where the Kerry Way has been routed up a stony track. As you follow this track around the slopes of Drung Hill, there is a series of gates and stiles between the fields. Later, however, the track occupies a notch cut from the steep, heathery slope and there are sweeping views along the coast and across Dingle Bay, possibly featuring Brandon Mountain under a woolly cap of cloud. The track crosses a little gap on the slopes of Drung Hill, then runs gradually downhill to pass through a forest on the slopes of Beenmore. After

A dead straight bog road takes the Kerry Way towards Cahersiveen

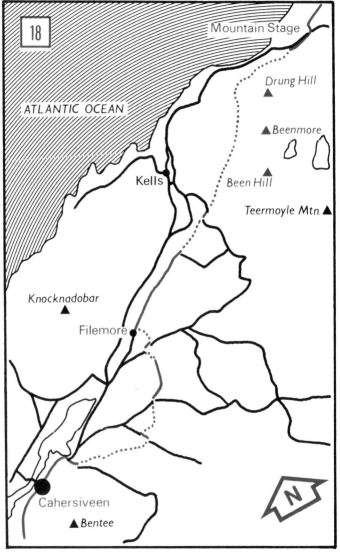

leaving the forest, the track proceeds over a slight rise, then runs downhill again passing a series of small, ruined cottages on the lower slopes of Been Hill. The track finally runs into a minor road, which you follow by heading off to the left. When the road later turns left itself, you need to drop off to the right and forge across a rugged patch of ground following marker posts. A muddy old track leads onwards, and this runs down onto a lower road. Simply walk straight ahead on this minor road until you are close to Filemore Church.

A left turn at Filemore leads along an old Mass Path which is equipped with kissing gates as it crosses a couple of fields and two rivers. When you reach the next road, turn right and follow it a short way, then turn left and walk uphill a short way. Turn right to follow an old track and follow this line to the next minor road. Turn left to follow this road past a number of small farms, until you reach a three-fingered Kerry Way signpost. Continue along the road, which is signposted for Cahersiveen (the other turning to the left would take you around the entire Kerry Way circuit). The road runs to a junction, where you continue straight onwards to follow a path across fields and downstream alongside a small river. The Kerry Way turns left along the next road, then right to leave it and head down to a footbridge spanning the Carhan River. An old bog road leads straight across a broad bogland, and at the end of it you turn right to follow a minor road down to the main N70 road just outside Cahersiveen. You should look out for a ruined, ivy-clad building by the roadside, which was the birthplace of Daniel O'Connell. By turning left along the main road, you'll soon be in Cahersiveen, though it is a long and straggly little town which takes some time to pass through. There are plenty of shops, pubs and lodgings on offer, as well as a Tourist Information Office in an old barracks.

Mountain Stage

The name refers to the time when horse-drawn coaches were hauled around the mountainside from Glenbeigh to Cahersiveen. It was customary for horses to be changed at stages for fresh teams, and hence the Mountain Stage was the point where the team climbing from Glenbeigh would be changed for another team who would take travellers around the mountainside. The high-level track used by the Kerry Way was the old road used by horse and coach transport. This was later replaced by the lower minor road, offering an easier course. A railway was cut around the mountainside, though after its closure the trackbed was converted into a road. This is now the main N70 Ring of Kerry road, which carries luxury coach traffic from around the world. As you progress around the steep slopes of Drung Hill, you should be able to pick out all these varied routes around the mountain.

Cahersiveen

One of the first structures noticed on the outskirts of Cahersiveen is a ruined, ivy-clad building which was the birthplace, in 1775, of Daniel O'Connell. He was known as "The Liberator" and his impressive monument was seen at the start of the Coast to Coast Walk on O'Connell Bridge in Dublin - which seems like a whole world away! Once you reach Cahersiveen, the waymarked stretch of the Kerry Way ends suddenly. It is in any case only a spur route offering walkers a chance to avail themselves of a full range of facilities as they trek around the Iveragh peninsula. You could choose to end the Coast to Coast Walk here, by walking down to dip your feet in the tidal Valencia River, but it's worth continuing onwards to end on a splendid Atlantic headland. However, go down to the Valencia River anyway, to see the Old Barracks which is also the Tourist Information Office. This structure is almost Disney-esque in appearance and has been reconstructed from the shell which was left after the building was burnt in the 1920s. You should remember to enquire about ferries to Valencia Island from Renard Point. It may be necessary to phone ahead and make an arrangement with a boatman to take you across, as there is no specific ferry schedule. Bus Eireann table number 179 offers a link with Killarney and Tralee, with no Sunday service, while table number 178 offers a Ring of Kerry service linking with Killarney and Tralee only in the summer. You should bear these bus services in mind as there are no buses serving Valencia Island, so you may also wish to make some arrangements to be collected and possibly brought back to Cahersiveen after the end of the Coast to Coast Walk tomorrow.

The old barracks at Cahersiveen has been completely restored

117

DAY 21:
Cahersiveen to Bray Head
(Sketch map 19)

Distance: 13 miles (21km).

Maps: OS 1:50,000 Sheet 83.
OS 1:126,720 Sheet 20.

The final stretch of the Coast to Coast Walk has no waymarks, but simply makes use of an obvious series of roads to progress the walk to a scenic and interesting conclusion on the sub-tropical Valencia Island. Leave Cahersiveen by following the main N70 road out of town, passing the Meteorological Station. At Renard Cross you should turn right and walk along a minor road down to Renard Point. There is a quay here, as well as the Point Bar in case of inclement weather while you wait for your ferry. You might as well dip your feet in the sea at this point, as you certainly won't be able to do so at Bray Head later. In any case, this is as far as the walk comes on the mainland - after this you are walking across Valencia Island.

The short ferry crossing leads to the little village of Knightstown, where you should turn right to face a clock tower. Turn left up another road, then bear right at a fork in the road at a church. Another minor road runs gradually uphill and passes a ruined church. As it proceeds further, luxuriant growths of rhododendrons and other plants flank the road and almost completely enclose it. After emerging from the vegetation cover, turn sharply left, then right, along other narrow roads. Open views take in a substantial part of the island, and you should also be able to spot the bridge linking the island to the mainland at Portmagee. Simply follow the road straight onwards, avoiding any turnings to the right or left. A series of houses and small farms is passed as the road gradually descends, and you should also notice a standing stone off the road to the left.

Journey's end can be seen ahead in the distance, where a tower

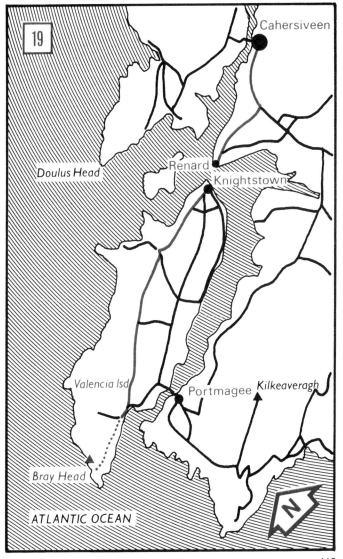

stands on the shoulder of Bray Head. The road you are following runs down to a junction amid a plantation of palms, where a right turn is required. A small car park is later found on the left, where a gate gives access to a track. The track, you will have noticed on the approach, runs straight up the grassy slope to the old Marconi Tower on Bray Head. This is situated at an altitude of 178m and offers fine views along the Kerry coast. Far below is the restless Atlantic Ocean, and various sea-birds wheel around the rugged cliffs. This is a scenic and dramatic conclusion to the Coast to Coast Walk across Ireland.

The day's walk is short, so you will have time to stand, or sit, and reflect on the long journey. You can gaze out across the ocean, or along the coast, or back inland - remembering the long walk and its varied scenery and experiences. You will, of course, have to leave this airy perch at some point and you should walk back down the track to the road. By keeping to the right at any junctions, you will be led across the bridge linking Valencia Island with the little village of Portmagee. You could enjoy a final snack or drink at a pub, or visit the Skellig Experience Visitor Centre, which could include a cruise around those mysterious islands if you can spare the extra time. There is no public transport, so you should be prepared to arrange for a lift back at least to Cahersiveen. Whatever you do at the end - the Coast to Coast Walk is over.

HIGH LEVEL ALTERNATIVE ROUTES

The waymarked trails which make up the Coast to Coast Walk are generally routed through fairly low-lying countryside. The Wicklow Way does in fact climb to heights above 500m and 600m in places, but the other trails rarely rise to 500m and generally stay much lower. Long distance walkers will sometimes find themselves following a minor road or forest track along the foot of a range of high mountains, and they may wonder if there are any routes which would take them across the distant summits and through wilder landscapes. There are in fact many places where you could enjoy high-level alternative routes, but you should remember that these are not waymarked routes, so you do your own navigating and route finding; nor do they carry any right of access, so you must be on your best behaviour and be prepared to leave if requested by the landowner; and you should bear in mind that these routes could prove most difficult to negotiate safely in foul weather. A total of eight alternative routes is offered for competent hillwalkers, but the route details are given only in outline form. You will have to find your own way from summit to summit using map and compass where necessary. You should take great care not to cause any damage when you find walls or fences across your route and no stiles or gates.

Routes such as the Lug Walk or the walk along the crest of MacGillycuddy's Reeks are recognised classics. Routes along the Blackstairs, Comeragh and Knockmealdown Mountains, or the circuit of the Coomsaharn Horseshoe, are slowly becoming more popular as more walkers take to the hills. The traverse of Caherbarnagh and The Paps, by contrast, is seldom attempted as a day walk, though The Paps do attract a number of walkers in their own right. Similarly, the route offered over Crohane and Mangerton Mountain suffers from the exceptionally difficult terrain which needs to be crossed on the way up Crohane, as well as the rugged

THE IRISH COAST TO COAST WALK

country beyond, although Mangerton Mountain and the circuit of Glennacappul is actually quite popular. All the high-level routes are described so that you can see where they break off from the waymarked trails, and how they link back into the trail network afterwards. You may need to alter the suggested daily schedule outlined in the guidebook in order to incorporate some of the high-level options into the Coast to Coast Walk, and you may find that your choice of accommodation might be limited to the first lodgings you reach if you are descending tired and hungry from the mountains late in the evening. Hardy hillwalkers should be able to complete most of the high-level routes within a day, but the Lug Walk is perhaps too long and arduous for most walkers to complete in a day and the course should be covered over two days at least.

The Lug Walk

Maps: OS 1:50,000 Sheets 56 and 62.
         OS 1:63,360 Map of Wicklow District.
         OS 1:126,720 Sheet 16.

The Lug Walk is a Wicklow Mountains classic, but any attempt to cover the distance should be based on a rigorous assessment of your stamina and abilities - to say nothing of the weather and the number of daylight hours. The true course of the Lug Walk can be adapted to take the place of the Wicklow Way as described on Day 3 and Day 4 of the Coast to Coast Walk, or from Knockree Youth Hostel to Aughavannagh Youth Hostel. In fact, you could do yourself a favour by staying at Glencree Youth Hostel before embarking on this alternative, and as the distance from Glencree to Aughavannagh is 35 miles (56km), you may wish to break half-way by descending from the Wicklow Gap to Glendalough Youth Hostel. This adds another 10 miles (16km) to the overall distance. Be warned that the Lug Walk crosses the most desolate, bleak and boggy parts of the Wicklow Mountains, where progress is hampered by decaying blanket bogs which are cut into an awkward series of hags and groughs. The altitude range is from 400m to 925m, and there are no habitations or facilities of any kind along the way. The only roads crossed are on the Sally Gap and Wicklow Gap - two of the highest roads in Ireland.

Route Outline

Leaving Glencree Youth Hostel and the former barracks buildings behind, follow the road a short way uphill, then start to climb up the rugged slopes above the road. At the top of the slope, keeping well away from the cliffs fringing Lower Lough Bray, the summit TV mast on Kippure can be seen in clear weather. Aim towards this obvious feature, crossing difficult ground which begins to steepen as the TV mast is approached. The 757m summit is the highest point in Co Dublin, though as you cross over the rather worn-looking summit you will cross the county boundary into Co Wicklow.

No-one would blame you for following the access road downhill from the TV mast, which would save you a difficult slog across the southern slopes of Kippure. The access road links with the R115 road at a clump of bushes, and this road is also known as the Military Road. Follow it across Liffey Head Bridge and continue to the crossroads on the Sally Gap. Climb up the steep slope south-west of the gap, which is clothed in deep heather. A reasonably clear path is soon encountered, which traces the course of an old boundary ditch uphill. The stony trough of the ditch offers a fairly firm footing and leads to the 682m summit of Carrigvore, where a few boulders litter the moorland waste.

Boggy patches are crossed as the boundary ditch descends from Carrigvore. After crossing a gap, there is a two-stage ascent of Gravale, which is separated by a level area of bog. The 718m summit has a cairn, though there are also some large boulders around. After leaving the summit, the descent passes more large boulders on the slopes of Gravale, then walkers continue down a rugged slope to land on a broad, boggy gap. A steep slope rises beyond the gap, and the ground is rather wrinkled and proves difficult underfoot. It is at this point that you may wish you were following the Wicklow Way over Djouce Mountain instead! However, the 720m summit of Duff Hill is easier to cross and it bears a cairn and a few boulders. Views in all directions appear to be quite desolate.

There is an easy descent from Duff Hill and this high-level route keeps to the crest of the range to cross another broad gap. The next ascent is fairly gentle, and as the blanket bog has washed away in places, you can walk up a stony slope which offers a firm, dry surface. As you follow the broad moorland crest uphill, a minor rise is crossed on the way to the summit of Mullaghcleevaun East at around 790m. Large granite blocks occur there, as well as a cairn. A descent westwards from Mullaghcleevaun East leads across a broad area of black peat. There is little vegetation cover to bind the surface so you should try and outflank the softer parts, particularly after wet weather. A broad shoulder leads ever upwards towards the top of Mullaghcleevaun. The summit trig point stands at 849m in an area of short grass broken by a number of large boulders. One of the rocks has a memorial fixed onto it recording a drowning tragedy on Cleevaun Lough which can be seen below the summit. Splendid views in all directions reveal something of the extent of the Wicklow wilderness.

Heading southwards from Mullaghcleevaun, note that the moorland crest swings south-east before you can proceed directly towards the little hump of Barnacullion at 714m. The ground is a mess of peat hags and groughs in places, and many walkers who started in the hope of reaching Aughavannagh in daylight may begin to despair at this point. By keeping east of the moorland crest beyond Barnacullion, however, you can walk along a feature known as the Green Road - where the blanket bog ends abruptly above the steeper slopes of the mountain. More rapid progress can be made towards Tonelagee, which is climbed in two stages. First a 714m summit is gained, then a slight descent leads across a stony gap, before another steep pull up to the 817m summit of Tonelagee. There is a trig point and cairn, while the view towards distant Lugnaquillia may be sufficient to make most walkers want to break the journey soon, rather than risk a possible benightment in the heart of the wilderness.

Descend roughly south-west to reach the R756 road on the Wicklow Gap. If you don't intend continuing this rough, tough walk in the remaining daylight hours, or even into the night, then follow the road down through the lovely Glendassan and stop for the night at Glendalough. In the morning, you can either resume the high-level walk through the wilderness, or switch to the easier course of the Wicklow Way.

Walkers who are game for more thrashing about in the upland bogs should return to the top of the Wicklow Gap and follow a narrow tarmac road to the summit of Turlough Hill. This is a strange summit, dominated not by a shapely peak and cairn, but by a reservoir and a concrete tower - all part of a hydro-electric Pumped Storage Scheme. Despite the blight on the wilderness, this feat of engineering is popular with visitors and minibus rides are sometimes offered up the road to the reservoir! Purist walkers can move away from all this and settle for a nearby summit at 681m which has a more natural appearance.

In mist, the next section can be particularly tricky, as there is no path, plenty of bog, and only the little Lough Firrib is an aid to navigation. From the lough, you can either head south-west to gain the 734m summit of Conavalla, or simply omit the summit and pass the Three Lakes on the way to the 701m summit of Table Mountain. This is an area of almost level black peat, but there is a small summit cairn in the midst of it all. As you head roughly southwards from the summit, you will cross the course of the Table Track near a prominent warning notice erected by the Army.

On the walk towards Lugnaquillia, you are actually progressing around the perimeter of the Glen of Imaal Artillery Range. There is no danger, provided that you don't drift eastwards into the glen. A few waymark posts have been planted over Camenabologue, and as most of the blanket bog has gone from the hill, the ascent is on a firm surface and the 758m summit is easily reached. There is a large summit cairn. By descending slightly east of south, a broad, hummocky gap will be reached.

Once across the gap, a staged ascent leads first to the little hump of Cannow Mountain at 712m, then along a broader crest which finally snakes towards the summit of Lugnaquillia. There is a useful path, which is handy as the summit of the mountain is quite broad, flat and grassy. A trig point stands at 925m and there is also a large platform cairn. A view indicator helps walkers to sort out a host of distant features. To make the most of the views, you should walk around the edge of the summit plateau, and in particular look over the cliffs of the North and South Prisons. Lugnaquillia is the highest point in Co Wicklow and the Province of Leinster.

To descend towards Aughavannagh and stay free of forests, use the following route. Walk a short way west of Lugnaquillia's summit cairn, then descend steeply south-west to reach a level gap of black peat. Beyond this, a short ascent leads to the 759m summit of Slievemaan. Leave the summit cairn and descend south-east, before swinging southwards along the heathery crest to reach the little hump of Lybagh. Continue descending south-eastwards to reach the edge of a forest, then follow the forest fence for a while. Move away from the forest and follow a track down towards a solitary farm in the Ow Valley. The farm access road leads to a minor road, where a left turn leads towards Aughavannagh Youth Hostel. You can lick your wounds as you travel along the Wicklow Way for the next couple of days, hopefully building up your strength for the next high-level alternative.

The Blackstairs Mountains

Maps: OS 1:50,000 Sheet 68 (not yet published).
OS 1:126,720 Sheet 19.

A walk along the length of the Blackstairs Mountains can be used to offer walkers a high-level alternative to the South Leinster Way between Kildavin and Graiguenamanagh. Most of that particular stretch of the South Leinster Way is either low-level, or routed largely along roads. The high-level route leaves Kildavin along the same course as the South Leinster Way, but keeps climbing to reach the summit of Mount Leinster, then runs across the Scullogue Gap to continue along the crest of the Blackstairs Mountains. After descending from the mountains near Glynn, walkers might as well head down to the tidal limit of the River Barrow at St Mullins and follow the Barrow Way towpath to Graiguenamanagh. The distance from Kildavin to Graiguenamanagh is 30 miles (50km) and unfortunately the only accommodation along the way is towards the end of the walk at St Mullins. This means that prospective walkers would need to cover at least 26 miles (43km) through the mountains before being able to break the walk in comfort.

Route Outline

Leave Kildavin in the company of the South Leinster Way, following a farm access road and forest tracks to climb between Greenoge and Kilbrannish Hill. The South Leinster Way follows a road up to the Corrabut Gap, then leads along the Mount Leinster Drive. After passing through a forest on this high road, walkers can leave the road and climb straight up the steep, heathery slopes of Mount Leinster. The going is quite difficult up the Black Banks, but it is a more natural line than using the access road serving the summit TV mast. The slope levels out for a while before a final pull up to the 792m summit of the mountain. There is a trig point and cairn on the summit, and despite the huge TV mast there are good views in all directions, looking back to the Wicklow Mountains and ahead to the Comeragh and Galty Mountains. The summit of Mount Leinster is the highest point in the counties of Carlow and Wexford, and also the highest point easily accessible to cars in Ireland, so you can expect to find plenty of company on top in clear weather.

The Carlow/Wexford county boundary is followed practically along the whole length of the Blackstairs Mountains to complete this high-level traverse. Descend from Mount Leinster in a southerly direction, picking a way down a steep and rugged slope. A series of old bog roads is now largely overgrown, but they lead further downhill and cross the eastern slopes of Knockroe. Allow yourself to be funnelled onto a stony track, which continues as a farm access road and leads down onto the Scullogue Gap. There are actually two parallel roads crossing the gap and you need to cross both of them to reach a small forest.

Use the forest track and a forest ride to reach the open slopes of Blackstairs Mountain. A steep climb leads uphill, then the gradient lessens and the slope is littered with thousands of boulders. The top of the mountains is an area of peat hags and the summit cairn at 730m rises above them. Head roughly south-westwards to descend, passing the huge blocks of rock known as Caher Roe's Den (Caher Roe being a robber of some repute). An old track is crossed on a gap, then a climb leads along the next length of the ridge.

Forests have been planted all along the eastern side of the Blackstairs Mountains, but by following the forest fence along the crest of the ridge you will generally have an open slope running down towards the broad vale of the River Barrow. Carrigalackan is the first summit on this part of the ridge, followed by Carrigroe and Dho Bran - the latter rising to 510m. As you descend further along the ridge, be sure to keep heading south-westwards along a spur of Dranagh Mountain. This spur is forested, but a prominent forest track leads quickly and easily down from the hills. The track runs into a network of minor roads before reaching the R729 road. This road can be followed towards the village of Glynn, from where you can walk down to the monastic village of St Mullins. Continue all the way down the road to the tidal reaches of the River Barrow. The towpath of the river has been waymarked as the Barrow Way and this clear path leads to the lovely little town of Graiguenamanagh, so that the South Leinster Way can be followed onwards to Inistioge.

The Comeragh Mountains

Maps: 1:25,000 Comeragh Mountains Map (not an OS Map).
         OS 1:50,000 Sheet 75.
         OS 1:126,720 Sheet 22.

The Munster Way merely toys with the fringes of the Comeragh Mountains, but this upland circuit travels through the very heart of the range. The shapely ridge of Knockanaffrin, which may be noticed on the forest walk above Kilsheelan, is traversed along its entire length. A prominent gap - known simply as The Gap - is crossed, before a steep climb leads onto the desperately boggy central plateau of the Comeragh Mountains. After thrashing and squelching a way along this broad crest, a descent is made towards the Nire Valley and a stretch of road-walking is required to pass through Ballymacarbry and link with the Munster Way again at Four Mile Water. The distance taken by this high-level alternative from the Munster Way at Harneys Cross Roads to the Munster Way at Four Mile Water is 22 miles (36km). There is an independent hostel near the start of the walk at Powers the Pot, and a choice of B&Bs is available in the Nire Valley towards the end of the walk.

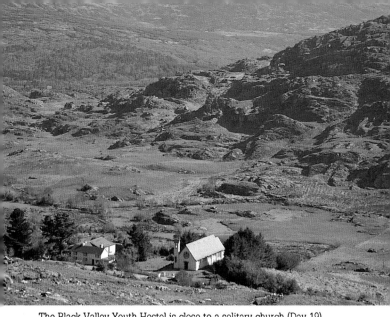

The Black Valley Youth Hostel is close to a solitary church (Day 19)

Bray Head - the end of the Coast to Coast Walk above the Atlantic Ocean (Day 21)

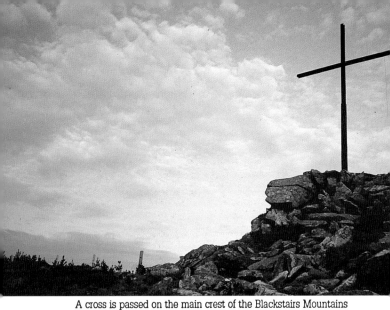

A cross is passed on the main crest of the Blackstairs Mountains
(Blackstairs Alternative)

Glenacappul - or the Horses Glen - is passed on Mangerton Mountain
(Mangerton Alternative)

Note carefully before attempting this walk that the boggy parts of the Comeragh Mountains really are very boggy and the walk should not be considered as an option after a period of heavy rain.

Route Outline
Head south-east from Harneys Cross Roads, following a minor road for a short way and crossing a bridge over a river. You now have easy access to the open ground leading towards the Knockanaffrin ridge. Be warned, this is a rough tract of country featuring deep heather, boggy patches and hidden holes full of water. However, if you set your face to the mountain and plod on steadily, progress uphill will gradually become easier. First, there is a steep and rugged climb onto the 535m summit of Shauneenabreaga. This is revealed as a small summit on the end of a spur and you will find this sort of feature repeated a couple more times as you continue to climb up the ridge. Beyond this line of false summits, the 675m summit of Knocksheegowna is more readily identified as there is a trig point lurking to one side of a peak of rock.

Continuing along the rocky ridge, descend to a grassy and bouldery gap which overlooks Lough Mohra. There is a steep and sometimes rocky ascent to the 755m summit of Knockanaffrin, which is marked with a cairn. Follow the ridge onwards, which descends in a series of huge steps. There are rocky areas amid the heathery slopes and a fence proves to be a useful guide in mist. The descent via the fence leads across The Gap, then a very steep climb commences. The frowning rock-face of Carrigshaneun is directly above, but you can outflank this obstacle to one side or the other. There is a level area beyond this rugged excrescence where you can pause for breath, then a somewhat gentler slope leads further uphill. A broad, stony area is reached, but as you descend towards a broad gap you will run into some desperately boggy ground. Chart careful diversions around soft patches, or aim to follow a stony channel uphill for a firmer footing. Either way, wet and boggy ground will need to be crossed in order to gain the broad summit of Fauscoum. There is a cairn at 792m, but to appreciate the views properly you should be prepared to walk around the edge of the boggy plateau, or simply gaze into the depths of the rocky Coumshingaun.

The bleak and boggy Comeragh plateau near the summit of Fauscoum

Charting a course along the broad and boggy crest of the Comeragh Mountains is paricularly difficult in mist, and there are few features in this wasteland of undulating blanket bog. However, if you walk north-westwards from the summit of Fauscoum, a broad and boggy gap is followed by a very gentle rise to a vast moorland hump. Head more towards the south-west now, to cross a rather more obvious boggy gap. A slightly steeper climb leads onto another moorland hump generally known as Coumalocha at 744m.

Technically speaking, Coumalocha is the name of a deeply entrenched corrie, and you can chart a course around its rim before crossing the broad and boggy crest which is perched between Coumalocha and Coumtay. At this point, you need to pick a course a little south of westwards to find a lengthy moorland spur which is the key to the descent. In misty conditions you should be aware that there are several changes of direction along this spur, but the idea is to cross the summits of Tooreen Mountain and Milk Hill as you descend. From the summit of Milk Hill, descend north-west down a steep slope and pick up a track which runs through the lower pastures and passes Knockavannie on the way down to a minor road. Simply follow roads into the Nire Valley and continue through Ballymacarbry to rejoin the course of the Munster Way at the tiny village of Four Mile Water.

The Knockmealdown Mountains

Maps: OS 1:50,000 Sheet 74.
OS 1:126,720 Sheet 22.

The Munster Way maintains a fairly low profile on the northern slopes of the Knockmealdown Mountains. The Avondhu Way climbs to greater heights on the southern slopes of the Knockmealdown Mountains, but still avoids the actual summits. The high-level option offered at this point is a complete traverse of the highest Knockmealdown summits, and this can be attempted between the village of Newcastle and Carran Hill in the Araglin Valley. The distance covered measures about 20 miles (32km), starting with a short stretch of the Munster Way, but ending in the company of the Avondhu Way. The Knockmealdown Mountains are largely covered in heather, with stony summits and a few boggy patches. In fact, they have the reputation of being among the driest mountain ranges in Ireland. The upland crest also bears a prominent stone dyke which is aligned to the county boundary between Tipperary and Waterford, which makes a useful guide along the main ridge. The open views from the ridge contrast markedly with the restricted prospects deep in the forest on the Munster Way. There is a prominent gap in the mountains which is known as the Vee Gap and at that point walkers could head off-route for accommodation either northwards to the little town of Clogheen, or southwards towards Lismore Youth Hostel. On a clear day the Knockmealdown Mountains offer remarkable views of the lofty Galty Mountains, which run roughly parallel.

The dry heathery crest of the Knockmealdown Mountains

Route Outline

Follow the minor road signposted for Mount Melleray Monastery, which leads away from the village of Newcastle. The Munster Way uses this road, but turns off to the right on the slopes of Knockroe. You need to continue following this road uphill to start this high-level option, crossing a gap and even heading downhill for a short while. There is a forest on the right and a track climbs up through it towards Knocknafallia. You will need to leave the forest at the end of the track, then climb very steeply uphill to gain the 668m summit of Knocknafallia. There is a shelter-cairn on top of the mountain which overlooks Mount Melleray Monastery.

Head roughly north-westwards to descend the stony and heathery slopes of Knocknafallia and cross a gap. Climb straight up the slopes of Knocknagnauv to find a stony embankment crossing three gentle swellings. The rise in the middle, at 655m, is the highest. The stone embankment offers a sure guide onwards, descending to a wide heathery gap which has some boggy patches. At that point, it diminishes into nothing more than a vague mound. You are also crossing the course of the Rian Bo Phadraig - the Track of St Patrick's

Cow - which climbs across the Knockmealdown Mountains on its way from the southern coast to the Rock of Cashel. The modern name for the waymarked trail is St Declan's Way.

Ahead is Knockmealdown itself and the stony banking forges straight up a steep, heathery slope to reach the 794m summit. Views from the trig point take in the Galty Mountains, Comeragh Mountains and Slievenamon, as well as vast tracts of lowland country. This is the highest point in Co Waterford, although the northern slopes fall into Co Tipperary. By following the embankment down from the summit of Knockmealdown, you will miss the summit of Knockmoylan, though you could include it in the route with a short detour. Similarly, the embankment swings suddenly left before reaching the 663m summit of Sugarloaf Hill. An ascent to the summit cairn offers a fine view of the Galty Mountains. A well-trodden and rather stony path descends the heathery slope alongside the embankment and lands on the R668 road which crosses the Vee Gap.

This road is a popular scenic drive, but walkers simply cross over it and pick up the course of the embankment for a rather steep ascent. This linear feature proves more difficult to follow now as deep heather and stunted rhododendrons get in the way. However, as progress is made uphill the vegetation cover gets shorter and the gradient eases. The banking becomes smaller on the upper slopes and suddenly veers off to the left. You can continue following a groove in the heather to reach a small summit cairn on an outcrop of rock. If you head southwards from the 630m summit of Knockaunabulloga, you will find the line of the embankment again, and now it is simply a peaty ribbon and as it proceeds across a gap it comes to look more like a stony path. In the end, you have to climb to the summit of Knockshanahullion without any aids to navigation. There is a trig point at 652m, as well as an enormous burial cairn and this has been fashioned into a shelter and heaped into a series of smaller cairns.

If you head southwards from the summit you will reach an area of turf cuttings and you can follow a bog road downhill in the company of the Avondhu Way. Stick to the course of the Avondhu Way as it crosses the next minor road and passes through a newly forested area. The waymarked route passes through a high gap

THE IRISH COAST TO COAST WALK

close to the two summits of Farbreaga. You can complete this high-level walk by climbing onto both summits, then follow the Avondhu Way down into the Araglin Valley. You may find a farmhouse B&B on the slopes of Carran Hill which would save you having to continue towards Fermoy for the night, but check in advance if this place is actually open.

The Derrynasaggart Mountains

Maps: OS 1:50,000 Sheet 79.
            OS 1:126,720 Sheet 21.

The Duhallow Way keeps fairly low across the northern slopes of Caherbarnagh and Knocknabro, then passes through a rugged gap between Knocknabro and The Paps. You could attempt a high-level walk over the summits of Caherbarnagh, Knocknabro and The Paps, and although this measures only 10 miles (16km) from Gortavehy to Clydagh Bridge, the terrain is quite rugged and the deep heather and tussocky grass could bring you to your knees. However, it's worth the effort to get to know the Derrynasaggart Mountains, which otherwise receive very little attention. Unfortunately, following this route would mean that you would miss seeing "The City" on the northern slopes of The Paps. In misty weather, or on a rainy day, you would be well advised to stay low and follow the course of the Duhallow Way, as the Derrynassagart Mountains are rather broad, bleak and featureless in many places, and the whole walk would be reduced to a mere exercise in navigation. The only accommodation options close to the route are at Millstreet and Clonkeen, so you will need to start by following the course of the Duhallow Way around Claragh Mountain, switch onto the high-level walk to reach Clydagh Bridge, then walk down through Clonkeen to search for lodgings. The high-level route from Millstreet to Clonkeen measures about 20 miles (32km) and is therefore a couple of miles shorter than the course of the Duhallow Way between the same two points. However, this is a rough and

The Paps - twin peaks rising above the rugged Derrynasaggart Mountains

tough alternative and it takes extra time and effort to complete.

Route Outline
The course of the Duhallow Way is followed from Millstreet, around the slopes of Claragh Mountain, down to Ahaphooca Bridge, then uphill towards Gortavehy. Don't swing right for Gortavehy Lough, but keep climbing up a steep slope to reach a broad moorland crest above. There is a little hump at 544m to cross on the ascent, then you could look over the rugged northern slopes to see Gortavehy Lough below a cliff face. A gentle climb leads to a prominent cairn on Stoukeen. By keeping to the broad moorland ridge, a hump is crossed at 627m on the way to the summit of Caherbarnagh. There is a trig point at 681m set back from a pronounced hollow in the mountainside.

You can follow a line south-westwards from the summit, then swing more to the west. This course roughly traces the line of the county boundary between Cork and Kerry, and there are the remains of an old fence to aid navigation. There are plenty of boggy patches, areas of heather, and vast growths of tussocky grass which

135

prove to be difficult on the way across a broad gap. After crossing the gap, a gently graded ascent proves to be quite arduous as the ground conditions remain awkward underfoot. Knocknabro has three summits, and a minor one is crossed on the way to the main one at 592m. A descent in a westwards direction leads down a steep slope which features deep heather, uneven ground and some bouldery terrain. However, the head of the rugged gap known as the Sloigeadal is reached and if you are exhausted you can use a clear track to head down towards the Clydagh Valley and a minor road.

There is a forest which has been planted on the top of the Sloigeadal and you can continue towards The Paps by climbing steeply uphill from the fence bounding the northern side of the plantation. There is some very deep heather to negotiate, but as you climb higher the vegetation becomes shorter. Given the shape of The Paps, which resemble two huge breasts, you won't really see the summits until you are quite close to them. The first one rises to 694m and bears a huge and prominent cairn which resembles a nipple in distant views. Continue westwards down a slope which has some stony patches and cross a gap. Climb up a heathery slope to reach the twin summit at 690m, which bears a trig point in addition to its nipple-cairn. There are splendid views towards the Kerry mountains and a choice of more high-level alternatives - but first there is a descent to make.

Follow the spur which leads southwards and descends in two stages to two more level parts of the crest. Turn right on the second crest and head more towards the west. At Derrymaclavlode you can pick up a track which runs down to a farm near Clydagh Bridge. After crossing the bridge, follow the main N22 road through Clonkeen and either settle for a B&B or head for Loo Bridge Youth Hostel.

Crohane and Mangerton Mountain

Maps: OS 1:25,000 Killarney National Park Map.
             OS 1:50,000 Sheets 78 and 79.
             OS 1:63,360 Map of Killarney District.
             OS 1:126,720 Sheet 20.

There isn't yet a waymarked link between the Duhallow Way and the Kerry Way, so a section of easy road-walking is described in this guidebook. Walkers who would like to attempt a high-level route to link with the Kerry Way are warned that some of the ground covered in the following description is exceptionally rugged. Bearing this in mind, it is possible to leave Loo Bridge Youth Hostel and make a direct assault on Crohane, but you will most likely pay for it in blood, sweat and tears. However, things get a bit easier beyond Crohane, though the rugged stump of Bennaunmore is an awkward obstacle. If you persevere and make an ascent of Stoompa, then your rewards will be great on a clear day, as you can enjoy a fairly straightforward horseshoe walk around Glennacappul and the Devil's Punch Bowl on the flanks of Mangerton Mountain. All that remains is a descent to join the course of the Kerry Way. A direct descent to the Old Kenmare Road crosses some rather difficult country, while an easier descent to Muckross has the advantage of a clear path most of the way and a range of useful lodgings at the end. The distance covered by the high-level option between Loo Bridge and Muckross is 16 miles (26km). This may seem quite short, but be warned again that some of the country crossed on the early part of the walk is really quite difficult.

Route Outline

Starting from the road junction at Loo Bridge Youth Hostel, the ascent of Crohane proves to be exceptionally difficult. Somehow, you have to climb up past a large lump of rock at the road junction, and you will certainly need to use your hands to haul yourself over this first obstacle. The rocky terrain beyond rises in a series of rugged outcrops scattered with broken blocks. If you don't actually break a leg in a hidden crevice, then you will likely have your legs shredded by gorse and brambles in the thorny scrub. If you like a severe challenge, then this is as tough as it gets and you'll find that the terrain is difficult most of the way to the 425m summit of Carrigawaddra. Although the ground steepens greatly towards the summit of Crohane, the vegetation cover is much shorter and there are no more concealed barbs and holes. The summit of Crohane displays a narrow crest bearing a cairn at 657m and offers splendid views towards Mangerton Mountain.

Descend south-westwards on a steep slope which becomes more rugged as progress is made downhill. After crossing a rough little hump at 447m, pass between Lough Nabroda and Crohane Lake. Keep well to the south of Bennaunmore to avoid exceptionally rugged terrain and cross a neighbouring summit at 391m. There are no easy ways towards Lough Fineen and Stoompa, but there are a host of more difficult ways to make height towards Mangerton Mountain. However, you should use the steep climb to Lough Fineen as a way of proceeding towards Stoompa and Mangerton Mountain and try and take the rugged slope steadily. Be assured that things will get easier. A final pull leads onto the 694m summit of Stoompa, which is bouldery and heathery like everywhere else, and there is a summit cairn.

A path can be traced roughly southwards from the summit and this crosses a rugged little gap. Rather than keeping to the broad moorland crest, you should aim to stay close to the break of slope between the blanket bog and the rugged flanks of Glennacappul, or the Horses Glen. There are views into this rugged valley which take in three loughs - Lough Garagarry, Lough Managh and Lough Erhogh. You can climb all the way round the head of Glennacappul, or include a short detour to reach the summit of Mangerton Mountain. There is a stark contrast between the scenic detail of the rugged glen and the level blanket bog of the summit plateau. There is a trig point at 839m and if you are prepared to scout around the edge of the boggy plateau you will find some quite good views of the surrounding mountains, especially the jagged crest of MacGillycuddy's Reeks.

For the descent from Managerton Mountain, you can use the spur which separates Glennacappul from the Devil's Punch Bowl and enjoy being perched on the ridge between the two scenic hollows. A path can be followed on the northern side of the Devil's Punch Bowl as far as the outflowing stream. At that point there is a boggy path which follows a ruined boundary wall gently downhill across a broad moorland slope. Go through an old gateway and proceed along a firmer surface across the heather slopes. These rather featureless slopes would prove awkward to negotiate without this clear path, so follow it gradually downhill with confidence and ford a stream on the lower slopes. The track follows this watercourse downstream and you may need to detour around some overgrown stretches. There is also some boggy ground to cross before a car park is reached by a minor road. Turn right to follow this road, which is called the Queen's Drive, pausing later at a viewpoint which overlooks the celebrated Lakes of Killarney. Turn left at the end of the road and drop down quickly towards Muckross, the Killarney National Park and the first stretch of the Kerry Way. There are a number of places offering accommodation and you can retire to one of them, clean yourself up and apply some first aid to your lacerated legs!

MacGillycuddy's Reeks

Maps: OS 1:25,000 MacGillycuddy's Reeks Map.
                   OS 1:50,000 Sheet 78.
                   OS 1:63,360 Map of Killarney District.
                   OS 1:126,720 Sheet 20.

The traverse of the MacGillycuddy's Reeks is a recognised classic and it is perhaps the ulitimate mountain walk in Ireland. It can be brought into play as an alternative to the course of the Kerry Way through the Black Valley and Bridia Valley. Make no mistake about the high-level nature of this walk, as it actually crosses the summits of eight out of the ten highest mountains in Ireland. The jagged crest features several peaks above 900m and Carrauntoohil - the highest mountain in Ireland - attains a height of 1039m. As the range is fairly close to the Atlantic Ocean and is generally caught in a damp westerly airflow, there are usually clouds shrouding the highest summits. Careful navigation would be required in these conditions, although some parts of the ridge do bear a trodden path. There are also many steep and rocky slopes, and one part of the ridge really requires the use of hands for balance. In rain, some of the rocks become slippery and a crossing in foul weather cannot really be recommended. However, on a clear day, with ample time at your disposal, you could enjoy this magnificent high-level walk and could expect to cover 16 miles (26km) between the Black Valley Youth Hostel and the Climbers Inn at Glencar. Both ends of this high-level option tie in with the course of the Kerry Way, but it is unlikely that you would have the time to continue onwards to Glenbeigh, as you might expect simply by following the Kerry Way through the valleys.

Route Outline

Follow the Kerry Way away from the Black Valley Youth Hostel, then turn right up the rough road towards the Gap of Dunloe. You won't be going all the way through the gap, but you should leave the road and climb straight up the steep and rugged slope to reach the 464m summit of Drisean. This is revealed as a mere shoulder of Cnoc na dTarbh, which is in turn reached by following a gently graded and rather blunt ridge further uphill. The 655m summit is marked by large blocks of rock. Walk a short way downhill to cross a gap, then climb up a steeper and more rugged slope to reach the 731m summit of Cnoc an Bhráca. There is a tall cairn on top of this hill and a line of posts is arranged along its crest.

Walk along the broad crest of Cnoc an Bhráca, crossing a minor rise of 721m before descending to a gap. The path crossing the gap runs towards the prominent peak of Cruach Mhór and zig-zags up a steep slope of rock and heather. There are a couple of level steps on this climb where you can pause for breath. The 932m summit is quite unmistakable, as a huge wall-like structure has been built there and a niche has been recessed into it to hold a small statue. You will need to use your hands on the next part of the ridge, as there are shattered rocks to chart a course around and some rather exposed steps where care is needed. Pinnacles of rock can be circumvented by using a handful of trodden paths, and eventually the 939m summit of The Big Gun will be gained.

Another rocky ridge leads onwards down to a gap, which is

Cruach Mhór and the jagged crest of MacGillycuddy's Reeks

crossed fairly easily. The ridge leading up to Cnoc na Péiste is quite difficult in places, so walkers usually keep to the left to avoid serious problems. Care is needed, then a final steep pull leads to the 988m summit of Cnoc na Péiste. Things become much easier, though you may have spent more time scrambling along the ridge than you originally thought. The ridge-walk becomes quite simple and you will quickly be able to cross a grassy gap and make a short ascent to the 973m summit of Maolán Buí. A gently graded, but stony ridge runs down to another gap, then there is a very slight ascent to a summit at 926m, before the ridge dips down to the next gap. A slightly steeper ascent leads onto the grassy summit of Cnoc an Chuillin, which bears a cairn at 958m. A lengthy descent leads down a steep and stony slope, then runs out onto a grassy gap. The next ascent passes a ruined fence and appears to reach a summit, but you need to continue a little further along the broad and grassy crest to reach the true summit of Cnoc na Toinne at 845m.

Ahead is the great bulk of Carrauntoohil, but first there is a grassy ridge leading down to a gap at the head of the Devil's Ladder. This leaves walkers with a long and fairly steep climb to the summit.

The ground is both steep and stony in places, but the path is obvious and leads quite plainly to the summit. There is a trig point at 1039m, as well as a shelter-cairn and a huge metal cross which serves to make the summit unmistakable in distant views. Carrauntoohil is the highest mountain in Co Kerry, the Province of Munster and the whole of Ireland. If your ascent of Carrauntoohil is blessed with fine weather and clear air, then the views around the neighbouring mountains of Kerry are simply magnificent. If you find you have the time to spare for an "extra", then you might consider a scramble along the rugged ridge leading to Beenkeragh, returning to Carrauntoohil afterwards.

Taking care not to be drawn back down towards the Devil's Ladder, take a stony path down a fairly easy slope towards Caher. The path goes down to a narrow, rocky ridge where caution is required, though you can keep to a path across the southern side of the ridge and follow a safer line. A steep climb up from the ridge leads to a stance at a height of 983m, then you continue to the main summit of Caher at 1001m. Descend roughly south-west along a ridge, swinging more to the south to cross the little hump of Curraghmore at 822m. Continue the descent south-westwards again, noting that the ridge becomes more roughly vegetated and hummocky. As the ridge begins to swing to the west, it reaches the top of the Lack Road, where the Kerry Way crosses from the Bridia Valley towards Lough Acoose. By descending the rugged northern side of the gap, you can follow the Kerry Way past Lough Acoose and along the road to end at the Climbers Inn at Glencar. After your traverse of the "Roof of Ireland" it is unlikely that you would have the time to proceed to Glenbeigh for the night.

The Coomsaharn Horseshoe

Maps: OS 1:50,000 Sheets 78 and 83.
            OS 1:126,720 Sheet 20.

Coomsaharn is an exceptionally rocky hollow occupied by a large lake in a range of mountains some distance from Glenbeigh. The

Kerry Way only takes in the foothills and flanks of those mountains, crossing a low gap between Seefin and Coolroe to reach Glenbeigh, then crossing the slopes of Drung Hill, Beemore and Been Hill on the way to Filemore. If you were prepared to miss Glenbeigh and its facilities, then you could enjoy instead a remote high-level walk based on the Coomsaharn Horseshoe. The route suggested leaves the Kerry Way on the gap above Glenbeigh and climbs Coolroe first. The route then keeps as high as possible to cross all the mountain summits around the head of Coomsaharn. You could drop down from the heights at Been Hill and rejoin the Kerry Way, but to get the fullest enjoyment from the circuit it is recommended that you follow the crest of Beenmore and Drung Hill, then double back along the Kerry Way and head for a B&B at Filemore. This is the last chance on the Coast to Coast Walk to enjoy a high-level walk through an entire range of mountains, and the distance from Glencar to Filemore via the Coomsaharn Horseshoe is 22 miles (36km). The Coast to Coast Walk stays at a fairly low level as it continues towards its end on Valencia Island.

Route Outline
Follow the Kerry Way as if walking from Glencar to Glenbeigh, but switch to the high-level route on the top of the gap between Seefin and Coolroe. A short climb leads up the heathery slopes of Coolroe to the 414m summit of the hill. Descend southwards to a hummocky gap, then climb in stages towards Beenreagh. There is long grass and heather to hamper you on this broad, hummocky crest, as well as some boggy patches, but eventually the 495m summit of Beenreagh will be reached. There is a short, fairly steep descent to a broad gap, then this is followed by a longer and steeper pull up to the 607m summit of Macklaun. Beyond Macklaun is a long and broad ridge which draws walkers onwards, then a long spur leads uphill and around the precipitous slopes of Coomeeneragh to gain the 715m summit of Meenteog.

Follow the broad moorland slope downhill from Meenteog and trace an old boundary wall and ditch across the broad gap. This feature proves to be a useful guide over the next few summits, so walk alongside it and become familiar with its construction. Have a look over the edge of a steep slope into the rocky confines of

Coomsaharn. The wall and ditch runs uphill, but you will find that a boggy ditch and a line of fenceposts actually cross the 772m summit of Coomacarrea. The boundary ditch can be traced downhill, then a fence accompanies it across the next gap. Although the line of the ditch becomes rather vague, it can be traced around the head of Coomsaharn on the upper slopes of Teermoyle Mountain. A simple detour would enable the 760m summit to be visited, which is mostly composed of peaty areas and rashes of stone.

The boundary mound and ditch leads down a broad slope of stones and bare peat on the northern side of Teermoyle Mountain. A fence later runs across a broad gap and you can look down into the rugged hollow of Coomaglaslaw. The fence turns off to the left, but keep following the stony mound uphill and you will reach the 665m summit of Mullaghnarakill, where large slabs of rock can be found. The course of the boundary ditch runs across the eastern slopes of Been Hill, crossing a couple of small streams falling into Coomacronia. If you want to visit the 650m summit of Been Hill, then you will need to make a detour westwards.

Beenmore is the next summit in line and a stony mound leads straight up a steep and heathery slope. A shelter-cairn is passed on the way uphill, then the 669m summit is marked with a cairn. Continue along a narrow, heathery ridge which bears a path leading straight towards Drung Hill - the last summit on the circuit. Views from the 640m summit trig point and cairn take in ranges of mountains on both the Iveragh and Dingle peninsulas of Co Kerry. By heading roughly westwards, a very steep descent gradually eases and the rugged ground gives way to a track. Turn left and follow this track, which is revealed to be a part of the Kerry Way. Follow the Kerry Way onwards to reach Filemore, where you can find a B&B without having to go all the way to Cahersiveen. The series of high-level options is over and low-level tracks and roads lead onwards to Cahersiveen and the end of the Coast to Coast Walk on Valencia Island.

COAST TO COAST
ACCOMMODATION LIST

DUBLIN:
Numerous hotels, guesthouses, bed and breakfast and hostel accommodation. For full details, contact the Tourist Information Office, O'Connell Street, Dublin. Tel: 01 8734660.

KNOCKREE:
Knockree Youth Hostel. Tel: 01 2864036.

ENNISKERRY:
Enniscree Lodge Inn, Cloon. Tel: 01 2863542.
Powerscourt Arms. Tel: 01 2863507.
K. Lynch, Cherbury, Monastery. Tel: 01 2828679.
E. Cummins, Corner House. Tel: 01 2860149.
M. Clarke, Cregg House, Glencree Road. Tel: 01 2863557.
Summerhill. Tel: 01 2867928.

BALTYNANIMA:
G. Foy, Forest Way Lodge. Tel: 01 2818429.

ROUNDWOOD:
N. O'Brien, Woodside. Tel: 01 2818195.
M. Malone, Ballinacor House. Tel: 01 2818168.

ANNAMOE:
C. Hawkins, Carmels. Tel: 0404 45297.

LARAGH:
D. McCoy, Oak View. Tel: 0404 45453.
N. McCallion, Laragh Trekking Centre. Tel: 0404 45282.
D. Vambeck, Derrybawn House. Tel: 0404 45134.
P. O'Gorman, Ard Bracken, Ballard. Tel: 0404 45294.

M. Byrne, Cullentragh. Tel: 0404 45131.
Wicklow Way Independent Hostel. Tel: 0404 45398.

GLENDALOUGH:
Glendalough Hotel. Tel: 0404 45135.
Glendalough Youth Hostel. Tel: 0404 45342.

GLENMALURE:
Glenmalure Youth Hostel. No telephone.
Glenmalure Lodge. Tel: 0404 46188.

AUGHAVANNAGH:
Aughavannagh Youth Hostel. Tel: 0402 36102.

KNOCKANANNA:
N. Whelan, Hillview. Tel: 0508 71195.

TINAHELY:
B. Malone, Rosbane. Tel: 0402 38100.
Murphy's Hotel. Tel: 0402 38109.
A. D'Arcy, Orchard House, Coolruss. Tel: 0402 38264.

SHILLELAGH:
B. Osbourne, Park Lodge. Tel: 055 29140.

CLONEGAL:
M. Plunkett, Clonegal House. Tel: 054 77293.

KILDAVIN:
M. Owens, Sherwood Park House, Kilbride. Tel: 0503 59117.

BORRIS:
T. Doyle, Old Yard. Tel: 0503 73185.
S. Breen. Tel: 0503 73231.

GRAIGUENAMANAGH:
Anchor Guesthouse. Tel: 0503 24207.
J. Maguire, Aisling, High Street. Tel: 0503 24190.

Brandon View House, Ballyogan. Tel: 0503 24191.

INISTIOGE:
L. Rothwell, Nore Valley Villa. Tel: 056 58418.
M. Naddy, Ashville, Kilmacshane. Tel: 056 58460.

MULLINAVAT:
The Rising Sun. Tel: 051 98173.
A. Conway, Mount St Joseph. Tel: 051 98154.

PILTOWN:
M. Maddock, Kildalton House. Tel: 051 43196.
J. Walsh, Fanningstown House. Tel: 051 43535.

CARRICK ON SUIR:
The Carraig, Main Street. Tel: 051 41444.
Orchard House, Sean Kelly Square. Tel: 051 41390.
Cedarfield Country House, Waterford Road. Tel: 051 40530.

KILSHEELAN:
J. Boland, Highfield House. Tel: 052 33192.
Nagles Bar. Tel: 052 33496.

HARNEYS CROSS ROADS:
Powers the Pot Independent Hostel. Tel: 052 23085.

CLONMEL:
Hotel Minella, Coleville Road. Tel: 052 22388.
Brighton House, Brighton Place. Tel: 052 23665.
L. Deely, Beentee, Ballingarrane, Cahir Road. Tel: 052 21313.
R. Morrissey, Hillcourt, Marlfield Road. Tel: 052 21029.
T. O'Callaghan, St. Loman's, Cahir Road. Tel: 052 22916.
N. O'Connell, Benuala, Marlfield Road. Tel: 052 22158.
J. O'Reilly, Hill Crest, Powerstown Road. Tel: 052 21798.
J. Phelan, Cluain Ard, Melview, Fethard Road. Tel: 052 22413.
M. Whelan, Amberville, Glenconnor Road. Tel: 052 21470.
Clonmel Arms, Sarsfield Street. Tel: 052 21233.

BALLYMACARBRY:
E. Ryan, Clonanav Farm Guesthouse. Tel: 052 36141.
S. Wall, Hanoras Cottage. Tel: 052 36134.
M. Doocey, Nire Valley Farmhouse. Tel: 052 36149.

NEWCASTLE:
River Valley. Tel: 052 36105.
B. O'Donnell, Kilmaneen Farmhouse. Tel: 052 36231.

CLOGHEEN:
Vee Valley Hotel. Tel: 052 65254.
B. Moran, Ballyboy House. Tel: 052 65297.

ARAGLIN:
J. & J. Hickey, Barnahoun. Tel: 058 60007.

FERMOY:
The Grand. Tel: 025 31444.
M. Bartley, Avona, Pike Road. Tel: 025 32195.
M. Crowley, Ardvarna, Duntaheen Road. Tel: 025 31858.
C. Ramirez, Avonmore Country House, Mallow Road.
    Tel: 025 32568.
D. Regan, Danmar House, Ballyhindon. Tel: 025 31786.
P. O'Leary, Palm Rise, Duntahane. Tel: 025 31386.
R. Mulvihill, Mounteagle House. Tel: 025 32425.

BALLYHOOLY:
Castle Tavern. Tel: 025 39206.

MALLOW:
Springfort Hall. Tel: 022 21278.
Central Hotel, Main Street. Tel: 022 21527.
Hibernian, Main Street. Tel: 022 21588.
Longueville House. Tel: 022 47156.
S. Wright, Oakville, Dromore Drive. Tel: 022 22074.
S. Clifford, Ard-na-Laoi, Bathview. Tel: 022 22317.
B. Courtney, Rathmore House, Fermoy Road. Tel: 022 21688.

M. Walsh, Riverside House, Navigation Road. Tel: 022 42761.
M. Kiely, Hill Top View, Navigation Road. Tel: 022 21491.
K. Leahy, Leadon, Navigation Road. Tel: 022 21661.
W. O'Donovan, Oaklands, Springwood. Tel: 022 21127.
S. Buckley, Cortigan House, Tel: 022 22770.

BANTEER:
Roche's Country House. Tel: 029 56125.
Clonmeen Lodge. Tel: 029 56238.
Dunhallow Lodge. Tel: 029 56042.

MILLSTREET:
S. ni Cheilleachair, The Laurels, Minor Row. Tel: 029 70090.
J. Storm, Ballinatona Farm. Tel: 029 70213.

CLONKEEN:
Loo Bridge Youth Hostel. Tel: 064 53002.
E. O'Donoghue, Woodgrove Farm. Tel: 064 53010.
S. O'Donoghue, Salmon Leap Farm. Tel: 064 53005.
K. Spillane, Islandmore House. Tel: 064 53009.

MUCKROSS:
S. O'Neill, Airan Heights, Lough Guitane Rd. Tel: 064 32071.
B. Joy, Forest Haven, Lough Guitane Rd. Tel: 064 33757.
H. O'Connor, Torc Falls, Lough Guitane Rd. Tel: 064 33566.
G. & M. Fogarty, Osprey, Lough Guitane Rd. Tel: 064 33213.
E. Looney, Kiltrasna Farm, Lough Guitane Rd. Tel: 064 31643.
M. O'Donovan, O'Donovans Farm, Mangerton Rd.
    Tel: 064 32238.
L. Cronin, Crabtree Cottage, Mangerton Rd. Tel: 064 33169.
A. Larkin, Deerwood, Mangerton Road. Tel: 064 34898.

KILLARNEY:
Numerous hotels, guesthouses, bed and breakfast and hostel
accommodation. For full details, contact the Tourist Information
Office, The Town Hall, Killarney. Tel: 064 31633.

BLACK VALLEY:
    M. Tangney, Hillcrest Farmhouse. Tel: 064 34702.
    Black Valley Youth Hostel. Tel: 064 34712.

GLENCAR:
    Climbers Inn. Tel: 066 60101.
    B. Breen, Blackstones House. Tel: 066 61064.

GLENBEIGH:
    Falcon Inn. Tel: 066 68215.
    The Village House. Tel: 066 68128.
    Glenbeigh Hotel. Tel: 066 68333.
    D. Doyle, Glencurran House. Tel: 066 68133.
    J. Griffin, Ocean Star. Tel: 066 68123.
    N. O'Toole, Ocean Wave. Tel: 066 68249.
    D. Caulfield, Forest View. Tel: 066 68140.

MOUNTAIN STAGE:
    A. Mather, Sea View House. Tel: 066 68109.
    H. Fox, Foxtrot. Tel: 066 68417.

FILEMORE:
    O. & M. Landers, Fransal House. Tel: 066 72997.

CAHERSIVEEN:
    Ringside Rest, Valencia Road. Tel: 066 72543.
    N. McKenna, Mount Rivers, Carhan Road. Tel: 066 72509.
    M. Mahony, Castleview, Valencia Road. Tel: 066 72252.
    B. Landers, San Antoine, Valencia Road. Tel: 066 72521.
    T. Sugrue, Valencia View Farmhouse. Tel: 066 72227.
    C. O'Donoghue, Ocean View Farmhouse. Tel: 066 72261.
    M. McCrohan, Sea Front Farmhouse. Tel: 066 72357.
    Sive Independent Hostel. Tel: 066 72717.
    E. Dennehy, Sea Breeze, Renard Road. Tel: 066 726609.
    C. O'Neill, Iveragh Heights, Carhan Road. Tel: 066 72545.

KNIGHTSTOWN:
    M. Foran, Spring Acre. Tel: 066 76141.

J. O'Sullivan, Glenreen Heights. Tel: 066 76241.
Valencia Island Youth Hostel. Tel: 066 76141.

PORTMAGEE:
K. Lynch, Harbour Grove Farmhouse, Ahadda. Tel: 066 77116.
M. Lynch, Harbour Lights. Tel: 066 77172.
Moorings. Tel: 066 77108.

COMMON IRISH WORDS

Most of the placenames which appear on Ordnance Survey maps of Ireland are anglicised versions of the original Irish placenames. Sometimes, they have become so corrupted that the original meaning has been completely lost. However, Irish placenames are often highly descriptive, so that even a curious name such as Knockmealdown can be broken down into Cnoc Maol and Donn - which is another way of saying Bald Brown Hill. This is as good a description of the brown heathery slopes of the Knockmealdown Mountains as you will get - the rounded upper slopes being covered in "bald" stony tops. It is now the policy, as more and more 1:50,000 maps are being produced, to show some placenames in both the original Irish as well as in their anglicised forms. This list can be used to translate some of the placenames encountered on the Coast to Coast Walk, and may help to give a further insight into the country being traversed.

Irish Form	Anglicised Form	Meaning
Abhainn	Owen	River
Achadh	Augha	Field
Aill	Ail/All	Cliff
Ard	Ard	Height
Ath	Ath	Ford
Baile	Bally	Town/Townland
Bán	Baun/Bawn	White
Barr	Bar	Top
Beag	Beg	Small
Bealach	Ballagh	Pass/Gap
Beann	Ben	Mountain
Bearna	Barna	Pass/Gap
Beith	Beigh	Birch
Bóthar	Boher	Road
Bóthairín	Bohreen	Lane
Breac	Brack	Speckled

Irish Form	Anglicised Form	Meaning
Buaile	Booley	Summer Pasture
Buí	Boy	Yellow
Bun	Bun	Foot/End
Caiseal	Cashel	Stone Fort
Carn	Carn	Cairn
Carraig	Carrick	Rock
Cathair	Caher	Stone Fort
Ceann	Ken	Head
Ceapach	Cappagh	Plot of Land
Cill	Kill	Church
Cloch	Clogh	Stone
Cluain	Cloon/Clon	Meadow
Cnoc	Knock	Hill
Coill	Kil	Wood
Coire	Corry	Corrie
Cor	Cor	Round Hill
Corran	Carraun	Sickle
Cruach	Croagh	Steep-sided Hill
Cúm	Coom	Corrie
Dearg	Derg	Red
Doire	Derry	Oak Grove
Donn	Don/Down	Brown
Druim	Drum	Ridge
Dubh	Duff/Doo	Black
Dún	Dun/Doon	Earth Fort
Eas	Ass	Waterfall
Eisk	Esk	Steep Gully
Fionn	Fin	Fair/Clear
Fraioch	Freagh	Heath
Gaoith	Gwee/Gee	Wind
Garbh	Garriff	Rough
Glas	Glas	Green
Gleann	Glen	Valley
Gorm	Gorm	Blue
Gort	Gort	Field
Inbhear	Inver	River Mouth

Irish Form	Anglicised Form	Meaning
Inis	Inish	Island
Leac	Lack	Flagstone
Leacht	Lack	Large Cairn
Liath	Leagh	Grey
Loch	Lough	Lake
Log	Log/Lug	Hollow
Machaire	Maghery	Plain
Maol	Mweel/Meal	Bald
Mór	More	Big
Muc	Muck	Pig
Muillean	Mullin	Mill
Mullach	Mullagh	Summit
Poll	Poll/Poul	Hole/Cave
Rath	Rath	Earth Fort
Rí	Ree	King
Rinn	Rinn	Headland
Ruadh	Roe	Ruddy/Red
Scairbh	Scarriff	Shallow Ford
Sceilig	Skellig	Rock
Sean	Shan	Old
Sídh	Shee	Fairy Mound
Sliabh	Slieve	Mountain
Slí	Slee/Slea	Way
Spinc	Spink	Point
Srón	Sron	Nose/Spur
Stuaic	Stook	Pinnacle
Suí	See	Seat
Taobh	Tave	Side
Tír	Teer	Land
Tobar	Tubber	Well
Torc	Torc	Wild Boar

In addition, particles such as *an* or *na* can have the meaning of *the* or *of the*. Words ending in *ín* or *een* have the meaning of *little* - so that Stuaicín or Stookeen would mean Little Pinnacle.

CICERONE GUIDES
Cicerone publish a wide range of reliable guides to walking and climbing in Britain, and other general interest books.

LAKE DISTRICT - General Books

CONISTON COPPER A History
CHRONICLES OF MILNTHORPE
A DREAM OF EDEN -LAKELAND DALES
EDEN TAPESTRY
THE HIGH FELLS OF LAKELAND
KENDAL A SOCIAL HISTORY
LAKELAND - A taste to remember (Recipes)
LAKELAND VILLAGES
LAKELAND TOWNS
LAKELAND PANORAMAS
THE LAKERS
THE LOST RESORT? (Morecambe)
LOST LANCASHIRE (Furness area)
REFLECTIONS ON THE LAKES
AN ILLUSTRATED COMPANION INTO LAKELAND

LAKE DISTRICT - Guide Books

THE BORDERS OF LAKELAND
BIRDS OF MORECAMBE BAY
CASTLES IN CUMBRIA
CONISTON COPPER MINES Field Guide
THE CUMBRIA CYCLE WAY
THE EDEN WAY
IN SEARCH OF WESTMORLAND
SHORT WALKS IN LAKELAND-1: SOUTH LAKELAND
SHORT WALKS IN LAKELAND- 2:NORTH LAKELAND
SCRAMBLES IN THE LAKE DISTRICT
MORE SCRAMBLES IN THE LAKE DISTRICT
THE TARNS OF LAKELAND VOL 1 - WEST
THE TARNS OF LAKELAND VOL 2 - EAST
WALKING ROUND THE LAKES
WALKS IN SILVERDALE/ARNSIDE
WESTMORLAND HERITAGE WALK
WINTER CLIMBS IN THE LAKE DISTRICT

NORTHERN ENGLAND (outside the Lakes

BIRDWATCHING ON MERSEYSIDE
CANAL WALKS Vol 1 North
CANOEISTS GUIDE TO THE NORTH EAST
THE CLEVELAND WAY & MISSING LINK
THE DALES WAY
DOUGLAS VALLEY WAY

WALKING IN THE FOREST OF BOWLAND
HADRIANS WALL Vol 1 The Wall Walk
HADRIANS WALL VOL 2 Walks around the Wall
HERITAGE TRAILS IN NW ENGLAND
THE ISLE OF MAN COASTAL PATH
IVORY TOWERS & DRESSED STONES (Follies)
THE LANCASTER CANAL
LANCASTER CANAL WALKS
A WALKERS GUIDE TO THE LANCASTER CANAL
WALKS FROM THE LEEDS-LIVERPOOL CANAL
LAUGHS ALONG THE PENNINE WAY
A NORTHERN COAST-TO-COAST
NORTH YORK MOORS Walks
ON THE RUFFSTUFF 84 Bike rides in Northern England
THE REIVERS WAY (Northumberland)
THE RIBBLE WAY
ROCK CLIMBS LANCASHIRE & NW
THE TEESDALE WAY
WALKING IN COUNTY DURHAM
WALKING IN LANCASHIRE
WALKING DOWN THE LUNE
WALKING IN THE SOUTH PENNINES
WALKING IN THE NORTH PENNINES
WALKING IN THE WOLDS
WALKS IN THE YORKSHIRE DALES (3 VOL)
WALKS IN LANCASHIRE WITCH COUNTRY
WALKS IN THE NORTH YORK MOORS (2 VOL)
WALKS TO YORKSHIRE WATERFALLS (2 vol)
WATERFALL WALKS -TEESDALE & THE HIGH PENNINES
WALKS ON THE WEST PENNINE MOORS
WALKING NORTHERN RAILWAYS (2 vol)
THE YORKSHIRE DALES A walker's guide

DERBYSHIRE PEAK DISTRICT & EAST MIDLANDS

KINDER LOG
HIGH PEAK WALKS
WHITE PEAK WAY
WHITE PEAK WALKS - 2 Vols
WEEKEND WALKS IN THE PEAK DISTRICT
THE VIKING WAY
THE DEVIL'S MILL / WHISTLING CLOUGH (Novels)

Other guides are constantly being added to the Cicerone List.
Available from bookshops, outdoor equipment shops or direct (send s.a.e. for price list) from
CICERONE, 2 POLICE SQUARE, MILNTHORPE, CUMBRIA, LA7 7PY

CICERONE GUIDES
Cicerone publish a wide range of reliable guides to walking and climbing in Britain, and other general interest books.

WALES, WELSH BORDER & WEST MIDLANDS
ASCENT OF SNOWDON
THE BRECON BEACONS
WALKING IN CHESHIRE
THE CHESHIRE CYCLE WAY
CLWYD ROCK
HEREFORD & THE WYE VALLEY A Walker's Guide
HILLWALKING IN SNOWDONIA
HILL WALKING IN WALES (2 Vols)
THE MOUNTAINS OF ENGLAND & WALES Vol 1 WALES
WALKING OFFA'S DYKE PATH
THE RIDGES OF SNOWDONIA
ROCK CLIMBS IN WEST MIDLANDS
SARN HELEN Walking Roman Road
SCRAMBLES IN SNOWDONIA
SEVERN WALKS
THE SHROPSHIRE HILLS A Walker's Guide
SNOWDONIA WHITE WATER SEA & SURF
WALKING DOWN THE WYE
A WELSH COAST TO COAST WALK
WELSH WINTER CLIMBS

SOUTH & SOUTH WEST ENGLAND
WALKING IN CORNWALL
WALKING IN THE CHILTERNS
COTSWOLD WAY
COTSWOLD WALKS (3 VOLS)
WALKING ON DARTMOOR
WALKERS GUIDE TO DARTMOOR PUBS
WALKING IN DORSET
EXMOOR & THE QUANTOCKS
THE GRAND UNION CANAL WALK
THE KENNET & AVON WALK
LONDON THEME WALKS
AN OXBRIDGE WALK
A SOUTHERN COUNTIES BIKE GUIDE
THE SOUTHERN-COAST-TO-COAST

SOUTH DOWNS WAY & DOWNS LINK
SOUTH WEST WAY - 2 Vol
THE TWO MOORS WAY Dartmoor-Exmoor
WALKS IN KENT Bk 2
THE WEALDWAY & VANGUARD WAY

SCOTLAND
THE BORDER COUNTRY - WALKERS GUIDE
BORDER PUBS & INNS A Walker's Guide
CAIRNGORMS WINTER CLIMBS
WALKING THE GALLOWAY HILLS
THE ISLAND OF RHUM
THE ISLE OF SKYE - A Walker's Guide
THE SCOTTISH GLENS (Mountainbike Guide)
   Book 1:THE CAIRNGORM GLENS
   Book 2 THE ATHOLL GLENS
   Book 3 THE GLENS OF RANNOCH
   Book 4 THE GLENS OF TROSSACH
SCOTTISH RAILWAY WALKS
SCRAMBLES IN LOCHABER
SCRAMBLES IN SKYE
SKI TOURING IN SCOTLAND
TORRIDON A Walker's Guide
WALKS from the WEST HIGHLAND RAILWAY
WINTER CLIMBS BEN NEVIS & GLENCOE

REGIONAL BOOKS UK & IRELAND
THE ALTERNATIVE PENNINE WAY
THE ALTERNATIVE COAST TO COAST
LANDS END TO JOHN O'GROATS CYCLE GUIDE
CANAL WALKS Vol.1: North
LIMESTONE - 100 BEST CLIMBS
THE PACKHORSE BRIDGES OF ENGLAND
THE RELATIVE HILLS OF BRITAIN
THE MOUNTAINS OF ENGLAND & WALES
   VOL 1 WALES, VOL 2 ENGLAND
THE MOUNTAINS OF IRELAND
THE IRISH COAST TO COAST WALK

Also a full range of EUROPEAN and OVERSEAS guidebooks - walking, long distance trails,
scrambling, ice-climbing, rock climbing.

Other guides are constantly being added to the Cicerone List.
Available from bookshops, outdoor equipment shops or direct (send s.a.e. for price list) from
CICERONE, 2 POLICE SQUARE, MILNTHORPE, CUMBRIA, LA7 7PY

CICERONE GUIDES

Cicerone publish a wide range of reliable guides to walking and climbing abroad

**FRANCE, BELGIUM & LUXEM-
BOURG**
THE BRITTANY COASTAL PATH
CHAMONIX MONT BLANC
 - A Walking Guide
THE CORSICAN HIGH LEVEL ROUTE:
GR20
FRENCH ROCK
THE PYRENEAN TRAIL: GR10
THE RLS (Stevenson) TRAIL
ROCK CLIMBS IN BELGIUM &
LUXEMBOURG
ROCK CLIMBS IN THE VERDON
TOUR OF MONT BLANC
TOUR OF THE OISANS: GR54
TOUR OF THE QUEYRAS
WALKING IN THE ARDENNES
WALKING THE FRENCH ALPS: GR5
WALKING THE FRENCH GORGES
(Provence)
WALKING IN THE HAUTE SAVOIE
WALKING IN THE TARENTAISE &
BEAUFORTAIN ALPS
WALKS IN VOLCANO COUNTRY
(Auvergne)
THE WAY OF ST JAMES: GR65

FRANCE / SPAIN
WALKS AND CLIMBS IN THE
PYRENEES
ROCK CLIMBS IN THE PYRENEES

SPAIN & PORTUGAL
WALKING IN THE ALGARVE
ANDALUSIAN ROCK CLIMBS
BIRDWATCHING IN MALLORCA
ROCK CLIMBS IN MAJORCA
COSTA BLANCA CLIMBS

MOUNTAIN WALKS ON THE COSTA
BLANCA
THE MOUNTAINS OF CENTRAL SPAIN
WALKING IN MALLORCA
WALKING IN THE SIERRA NEVADA
WALKS & CLIMBS IN THE PICOS DE
EUROPA
THE WAY OF ST JAMES: SPAIN

**SWITZERLAND including adjacent
parts of France and Italy**
THE ALPINE PASS ROUTE
THE BERNESE ALPS
CENTRAL SWITZERLAND
CHAMONIX TO ZERMATT The Walker's
Haute Route
WALKS IN THE ENGADINE
THE GRAND TOUR OF MONTE ROSA
(inc Italy)
THE JURA - Walking the High Route and
Winter Ski Traverses
WALKING IN TICINO
THE VALAIS - A Walking Guide

**GERMANY / AUSTRIA / EASTERN
EUROPE**
HUT-TO-HUT IN THE STUBAI ALPS
THE HIGH TATRAS
THE KALKALPEN TRAVERSE
KING LUDWIG WAY
KLETTERSTEIG - Scrambles
MOUNTAIN WALKING IN AUSTRIA
WALKING IN THE BLACK FOREST
WALKING IN THE HARZ MOUNTAINS
WALKING IN THE SALZKAMMERGUT

Other guides are constantly being added to the Cicerone List.
Available from bookshops, outdoor equipment shops or direct (send for price list)
from CICERONE, 2 POLICE SQUARE, MILNTHORPE, CUMBRIA, LA7 7PY

CICERONE GUIDES

Cicerone publish a wide range of reliable guides to walking and climbing abroad

ITALY & SLOVENIA
ALTA VIA - High Level Walks in the Dolomites
THE CENTRAL APENNINES OF ITALY
CLASSIC CLIMBS IN THE DOLOMITES
THE GRAND TOUR OF MONTE ROSA inc Switzerland))
ITALIAN ROCK - Rock Climbs in Northern Italy
VIA FERRATA - Scrambles in the Dolomites
WALKING IN THE CENTRAL ITALIAN ALPS
WALKING IN THE DOLOMITES
WALKS IN THE JULIAN ALPS

MEDITERRANEAN COUNTRIES
THE ATLAS MOUNTAINS
CRETE: Off the beaten track
WALKING IN CYPRUS
THE MOUNTAINS OF GREECE
THE MOUNTAINS OF TURKEY
TREKS & CLIMBS IN WADI RUM, JORDAN
THE ALA DAG - Climbs & Treks (Turkey)

HIMALAYA & OTHER COUNTRIES
ADVENTURE TREKS - W. N. AMERICA
ADVENTURE TREKS - NEPAL
ANNAPURNA - A Trekker's Guide
EVEREST - A Trekker's Guide
LANGTANG, GOSAINKUND & HELAMBU - A Trekker's Guide
MOUNTAIN WALKING IN AFRICA 1: KENYA

ROCK CLIMBS IN HONG KONG
TREKKING IN THE CAUCAUSUS
CLASSIC TRAMPS IN NEW ZEALAND

GENERAL OUTDOOR BOOKS
THE ADVENTURE ALTERNATIVE
ENCYCLOPAEDIA OF MOUNTAINEERING
FAMILY CAMPING
FIRST AID FOR HILLWALKERS
THE HILL WALKERS MANUAL
LIMESTONE -100 BEST CLIMBS IN BRITAIN
MOUNTAIN WEATHER
MOUNTAINEERING LITERATURE
MODERN ALPINE CLIMBING
MODERN SNOW & ICE TECHNIQUES
ROPE TECHNIQUES IN MOUNTAINEERING

CANOEING
CANOEIST'S GUIDE TO THE NORTH EAST
SNOWDONIA WILD WATER, SEA & SURF
WILDWATER CANOEING

CARTOON BOOKS
ON FOOT & FINGER
ON MORE FEET & FINGERS
LAUGHS ALONG THE PENNINE WAY
THE WALKERS

Also a full range of British guidebooks to walking - from short family walks, day walks to long distance trails, biking, scrambling, ice-cllmbing, rock climbing and canoeing

---

Other guides are constantly being added to the Cicerone List.
Available from bookshops, outdoor equipment shops or direct (send for price list)
from CICERONE, 2 POLICE SQUARE, MILNTHORPE, CUMBRIA, LA7 7PY

PRINTED BY CARNMOR PRINT & DESIGN
95-97 LONDON ROAD, PRESTON, LANCASHIRE